Snapshot

Scenes and stories from the heartlands of Scottish football

To our pals
at Studio Something.
Enjoy the journey...
Dan./

Words by
Daniel Gray
Photographs by
Alan McCredie

nutmeg
The Scottish
Football Periodical

Supporters watch
Whitehill Welfare, at
Ferguson Park, Rosewell.

This book is a celebration of people and places. It is a love letter to the charms of football obscured behind tabloid screeching...

The main stand, Albert Park, Hawick Royal Albert.

...It is a mirror of we, the supporters. It is a portal into a different kind of Scotland. It is a documentary in print...

Radiate

Raith Rovers Ladies manager John Fettes gives his pre-match teamtalk before the home tie against Hutchison Vale

...Come with us, from Cowdenbeath to Eriskay, and from Gretna to Nairn. And bring a flask.

Snapshot

Scenes and stories from the heartlands of Scottish football

First published in Great Britain in 2020 by ARENA SPORT and NUTMEG

www.birlinn.co.uk
www.nutmegmagazine.co.uk

Text and image copyright © Alan McCredie, Ally Palmer and Daniel Gray, 2020

ISBN: 978 1 91375 900 1
eBook ISBN: 978 1 78885 374 3

The right of Alan McCredie, Ally Palmer and Daniel Gray to be identified as the authors of this work has been asserted by them in accordance with the Copyright, Designs and Patents Act 1988.

All rights reserved.

Every effort has been made to trace copyright holders and obtain their permission for the use of copyright material. The publisher apologises for any errors or omissions and would be grateful if notified of any corrections that should be incorporated in future reprints or editions of this book.

British Library Cataloguing-in-Publication Data
A catalogue record for this book is available on request from the British Library.

Designed and typeset by Ally Palmer, Palmer Watson Associates, Edinburgh

Typography
Logotype: Breve Display Regular
Body text: Acta Roman
By Dino Dos Santos
DSType Foundry. www.dstype.com

Cover image: All quiet on the western isles. No football at Eriskay FC. By Daniel Gray

Printed and bound by SIA, PNB, Latvia

Contents

The home front stoics

Daniel Gray

She walked how you imagine the largest Russian Doll in a set would walk. Rolling, almost. There was a tender sway to her movements, tilting smoothly from side to side. From each tree-bark hand hung a tea urn. Scottish football runs on tea. Tea in the Referee's Room, tea for the half-time player. Tea in foam cups, tea when you drop into a ground on a weekday afternoon. Tea to warm the winter, tea to show mistrust of fleeting summer and flighty warmth.

The Russian Doll heaved her urns up onto a table covered with a thick plastic tablecloth, its floral pattern wattle and daubed with empty sugar sachets and spilt milk. She wore a blue tabard with redundant pockets and sported a gently wise smile. "There you are, boys. That'll warm ye up before the second half. Take a biscuit too." She waddled away with that satisfied look women of her generation often display after they've fed and watered everyone else in the room and an "Och, I'll get something for myself later."

I see them at almost every ground I visit in Scotland, this quiet battalion. They are making and issuing tea as did the Russian Doll. They are rolling the pitch with feudal-era equipment and Sisyphean determination. They are shuffling tidy a pile of matchday programmes like a television newsreader as the lights fade. They are straightening their tie clips in the board room and removing cellophane from foil platter trays of tiny white sandwiches stuffed with grated luminous cheese.

I see them from border to island, from Junior to Highland. The amateur photographer with more camera gear than Latvian state TV, filing his pictures to be captioned with elaborations in a local newspaper. The PA announcer, folded sheet with names of sponsors and names of forwards in one hand, the intermittent and spluttering remote microphone in the other. The club historian ready to share the obscure, the every-game-fan with his nods from the players and the lotto seller jangling and cajoling. They are the home front stoics that make every club. These hardy thousands make football tick in Scotland, their hearts and their heads and their hands gone and given to the game. Every home match, they are there. Through the week, some keep the club ticking over, nightwatchmen and women, ensuring that our Saturdays have purpose, comfort and melancholy. No penny is frittered, no paper plate discarded unused. The football they nurture and prune is played in all sorts of homes: scraggy but loveable grounds with one grandstand; regal and bustling stadiums of noble vintage; characterful nook-and-cranny habitats with pillars blocking the view. Such places possess an altogether different kind of beauty, like disused rural limestone railway stations or fleetingly revealed ghost signs above mid-renovation shops.

This book is a celebration of all such people and places. It is a love letter to the charms of football obscured behind tabloid screeching. It is a mirror of we, the supporters. It is a portal into a different kind of Scotland. It is a documentary in print. Come with us, from Cowdenbeath to Eriskay, and from Gretna to Nairn. And bring a flask.

Capturing the heartlands

Alan McCredie

How do you photograph the mad world of Scottish football? Simple, really – just turn up and it gives you everything you need. From a photographer's point of view the game has so much to love, whether kids kicking a ball around in the park or floodlit midweek matches in front of sixty-odd thousand fans. Each is equally interesting to Dan and I. The contrasts are overwhelming and it is these that make photographing football, and Scottish football in particular, so compelling.

For these photo-essays Dan and I would

start off with nothing more than an idea, a rough itinerary of where to be and when, and that was about it. We would turn up and see what happened, and without fail we always managed to get *something*. People who run football clubs and teams are proud of those football clubs and teams and are always happy to show them off.

We spent long days driving round the unfashionable, yet distinctly picturesque, hinterlands of Scottish football, where the game remains much closer to its roots. We visited every level from the Juniors to the Premiership, and more. We followed the game through small towns and big cities, from municipal playing fields to the floodlit glare of Ibrox on a European night that would prove to be the final game of a curtailed season as the pandemic waited in the wings, ready to pounce.

There are no great secrets to these photo-essays other than the most simple ones of all – a love of football in all its forms and the desire to get up, get out, and be in the very muddy, insane, balletic, beautiful heart of it all.

Main image: Mural of Claire Emslie, Edinburgh.
Top: Relic of a 1,000 matches – sticking tape on the crossbar.
Bottom: Football in the park. The foundation of the football pyramid.

Chapter

The first day

August hope and fresh paint as the season begins

August has come again. Football is back. Such words sprinkle a Christmas Eve feeling upon us all. Interminable, domesticated Saturdays have departed and familiar, fixtured life can recommence. Resumed are our sacred routines – scarves sifted out and returned to necks, lucky routes taken, matchday pubs invaded for the first time since May, fortnightly acquaintances greeted again with quick enquiries of holidays and health, and engrossed conversations about players sold and signed.

Once more to the ground we go, inhaling sweet catering van scents as they hang in the air almost visible like the vapours in a Bisto advert. Back is the 50/50 draw and its faithful seller, as ever in a starchy raincoat and plukey beanie hat, and the neatly piled club shop, last season's away shorts in a £5 bin. The new shirt, modelled by full-kit child and corpulent granddad in crumpled weekend jeans, looks wonderful or awful and never in-between. Short sleeves are trusted by the kitted and the rest, for the first day is always sunny, is it not? Even an angry God couldn't drop rain on our August day of hope.

In pastoral Dingwall and briny Arbroath, in resurgent Dundee and solid Mount Florida, at scholarly Ibrox and folksy Firhill, and at charming Somerset Park, the hopeful gather. They share the same darting hearts as those assembling in Cowdenbeath, Dunfermline, Alloa, Falkirk, Gorgie and Perth. For the football supporter, this is a carnival day.

While the familiar comforts us, spying difference is a first day ritual of its own. A revamped matchday programme with its cryptic, initialled and hashtagged new name comes with a 50p price rise. Fences, fittings and awnings have been painted, cherished turnstile lettering covered and superseded. Even a change at the food hatch is noticed – perhaps promotion has been met with a new pastry supplier, relegation with staff losses. Soon will come the joy of sighting the pitch once more, our Lincoln Green meadow, staggeringly vivid as if last season we were watching in black and white. Then, the appraisal of new signings, their gait and first touches evidence enough to make an absolute judgement.

These themes are to be cherished as part of football's universality. Across this country and others, we are all feeling the hope and sniffing the Dulux. Year and place are hardly of consequence, no matter the changes in the game, the world and our lives. In Dunfermline and Gorgie, the pulse quickens when a chant is called rustily back into use, just as it does in Southampton, Mansfield, Wolfsburg, Utrecht and Bologna. We have all come home.

At Central Park, the 2pm shutters roll upwards and the turnstile girls arrive with their cash floats. The public address system croaks into life – Chumbawamba then Kaiser Chiefs, of course – and a lone pair of clanking palms groggily clap tracksuited players onto the pitch. Soon here, there and everywhere, football will begin again, and the week will once more have an anchor.

One hour before the new season at Central Park, Cowdenbeath.

CENTRAL PARK
JUNCTION BAR
ADULT & CHILD
£14
CONCESSION
£6
Wee Jimmies Bar
The Glen Tavern
ADULT
£12
SEASON TICKET
CFC

Do not leave dirty kit
lying on the floor
Put your dirty kit in the
laundry bins provided
MERLIN
ELECTRO-PLATING LTD
SIVES
5
MILLER
6
RUTHERFORD
16
GLEN
10
GLENFIELD
AUTOCENTRE

The home dressing room. Central Park, Cowdenbeath.

COWDENBEATH F.C.
BLUE BRAZIL
THE BLUE BRAZIL SHOP
Club Office Opening Hours
Monday 9am to 1pm
Tuesday 9am to 4pm
Wednesday Closed
Thursday 9am to 4pm
Friday 9am to 1pm
Saturday 10.30am to 2.30pm (Home Matches Only)
COWDENBEATH

The Club Shop.
Central Park,
Cowdenbeath.

Ten minutes to three at East End Park, Dunfermline.

Opening the turnstiles at Central Park, Cowdenbeath.

Old strips for the new season. East End Park, Dunfermline.

HO

Home. This is Alloa, but football's home is wherever there is a scrap of grass and a ball.

The first penalty of the season is missed at East End Park, Dunfermline.

Hearts scarves for sale. Tynecastle Park, Edinburgh.

Heart of Midlothian welcome back the fans for the first game of the season.

Outside Falkirk Stadium Jason Cummings of Hibs poses with two young fans.

Another top-flight season begins for St Johnstone at McDiarmid Park, Perth.

The season begins. Opening up at East End Park, Dunfermline.

Matchday is back and the doors are open once again at Marv's Emporium & Tearoom in Dunfermline Athletic's East End Park.

A 4-0 defeat at Alloa and a long journey home for this Peterhead supporter.

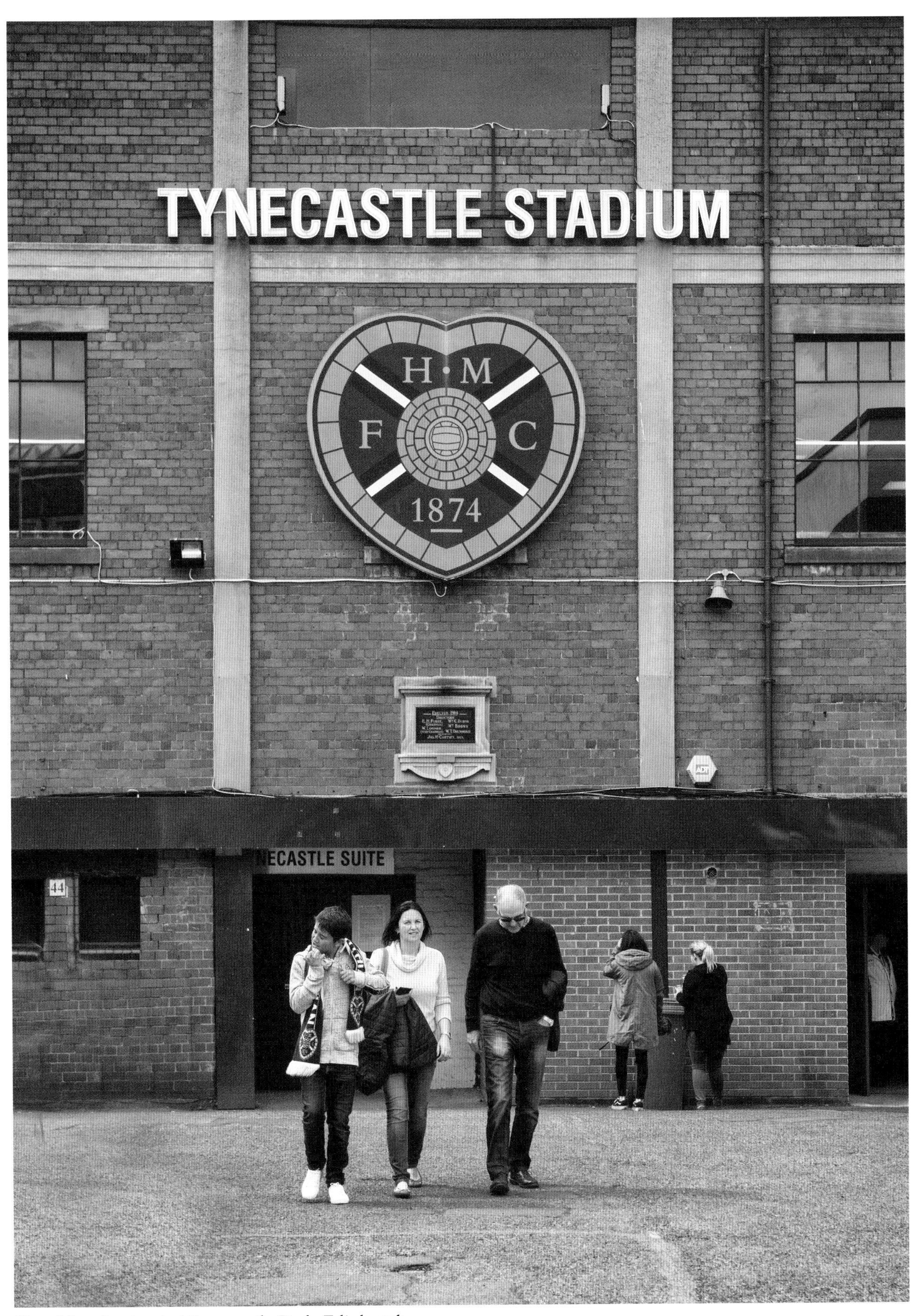

The old main stand at Tynecastle Park, Edinburgh.

Chapter

One lighthouse beamed, the other sighed

A North Sea yarn of exultant Cove and inconsolable Berwick

The North Sea spins yarns of heaven and hell. Joyous childhood holidays recalled and fishing boats tossed ragged. Beach versus lifeboat, amusement arcade versus tempest. Light and dark.

From May 2019, another verse of this conflicting shanty could be added: the exultant Rangers of Cove and the inconsolable of Berwick. Over two Saturdays in the middle of that month, Highland League Cove gutted League Two Berwick 4-0 and 3-0. Two lashings set to the soundtrack of North Sea seagulls high on waxy chips. 7-0 on aggregate, that by turns eulogising and murderous word. In one ocean settlement they raised their arms to the briny air; in the other they dropped their heads towards the sand. One lighthouse beamed, the other sighed.

This was the pyramid play-off game. By the end of the tie, Cove were at the apex, looking across a balmy hinterland. Berwick were in the burial chamber, mummified. Their 54 years of league football had ceased. The only English club in Scottish professional football would become the only English club in the Scottish Lowland League. Cove, fat on seven Highland League championships and not a little meat and gravy from oily Aberdeen, were taking their place. The past versus the future.

Days slid by and summer visited, bringing focus to ambitious Cove and easing Berwick's pain. By the season's eve, Cove were the bookies' favourites to be promoted again. Berwick supporters awoke to find that their club was still their club, that still they loved it so, whatever the name of the division. It was just as well; pre-season rained peltings of five, six and seven by Livingston, Stranraer and Ayr.

Turnstiles, Shielfield Park, home
of Berwick Rangers.

The artist L.S. Lowry adored Berwick-upon-Tweed. He holidayed here from the 1930s until the 1970s, painting matchstick and chimney scenes of this charismatic town. It is a shame that he never sketched Shielfield Park, Rangers' charming home since 1954, but not too much of a stretch to believe that he may have attended a fixture there. Lowry was, after all, a Manchester City fanatic and the creator of *Going to the Match*, surely the greatest artistic depiction of a football ground on game day.

Lowry only missed George Best playing at Shielfield by a few seasons, in one of those mind-bending near-collisions of seemingly disparate people, places and eras. The year of his last holiday by the North Sea was 1975, half a decade before Best's Hibernian were held to a 0-0 draw in a Scottish Cup quarter-final. Surely, though, Lowry knew of the little ground's most famous day – the 1967 defeat of Glasgow Rangers, in front of 13,365 people. "We have no complaints," said Blues captain John Greig, "we beat ourselves," half robbing the thrill of a hard-earned giant killing from the English side.

In 2019, we park on a grassy field behind the main stand. At its far end, young lads attend a football training session, oblivious in their Barcelona, Chelsea and Newcastle United shirts to the game beginning here soon. It is a shame for so many reasons, not least because at Shielfield, kids go free. No moaning here about families being priced out of football.

Conversation pitter-patters from the Black and Gold social club, and pints are held close to chests in the 1881 Bar. Behind one end of the ground whirrs the mighty Simpsons factory, purveyor of malt to brewers and distillers. Above and beyond, the sonorous ripple of trains approaching on the East Coast mainline makes a noise not unlike the

Ian and Rhona Beresford leading the line in the Berwick Rangers club shop.

rising tide of a busy football stadium just before a goal is scored.

Tonight, beneath this former BR railway track two other BRs are to meet for the first time – Berwick Rangers and Bonnyrigg Rose. Like Berwick and Cove, the away side find themselves in a new league after decades of Junior football. While it sometimes feels as though nothing changes at the top of the Scottish game, much is in flux and nothing is constant lower down. The Rose bring a buoyant away support through the shared turnstile. "Eeeee, you must be glutton for punishment" says a Berwick steward to a regular home fan. She giggles and mutters something about a life lived in hope.

Inside, the speedway track circumnavigating the pitch creates a wide and welcoming corner parish. It is a busy landing, like one of those genial small squares smattered with old men playing boules you stumble across on holiday. All the right human furniture is here – regulars talking of May gloom and promotion in ten months' time, lotto agents, programme sellers, kids tigging and messing. There is a queue towards the amber lights of the Bandits Snack Bar, named for Rangers' racing team cohabitors. Such sharing is a shivery reminder to all home supporters that in the 1980s Shielfield belonged to a greyhound promoter who evacuated their football club.

Of greatest appeal in this civic space is the club shop. It is impossible to enter and not feel that all is right with the world. Shirts, scarves, hats, badges, branded balls, programmes from seasons long forgotten on a rotating stand... In this breeze-block cabin are comforting, recognisable items; the threads of belonging and ritual.

Towards kick-off, a brew of middle-aged men in winter jackets begin to loiter. "Team lines in yet, pet?" one asks of Rhona, the friendly lady behind the counter. "Soon," she says, "soon," which provokes rolled eyes. Then, they arrive, 20 or so A4 sheets of line-ups and subs, officials' and sponsors' names, theirs for

The Berwick Rangers club shop.

20p a time. There is a scramble. One man buys five copies. They sell out in under a minute, and more are brought across from the main stand, provoking a mild, very British cheer. I must be far too besotted with football, because the whole thing makes me feel somewhat emotional. It has been a long summer.

Ian, Rhona's husband and fellow club shop volunteer, tells me all about his beloved club in the kind of Northumbrian accent that should be available on the NHS. Last season lingers. It froths out in key words and numbers: Bad luck; Star striker injured; 17 penalties conceded; Clyde's three point deduction; 33 players used to Albion Rovers' 44. To go down, finally, after so many seasons of survival was a shock. But here we are again, a glint in Ian's eyes and talk of going straight back up. Talk, too, of happy days gone by. Of Saturdays when it seemed like all the town was here. Of August matches singing "Back to school tomorrow" to visiting young fans of Scottish clubs.

On the pitch, as each club's season in a new division starts there will be more heaven and hell separating Berwick and Cove. The game at Shielfield begins in elegance. Above us is a salmon sky full of promise and poise. Rangers' black and gold stripes and Rose's red and white hoops please the eye. The turf is luscious, some kind of poem. Those stood in the Ducket, this ground's distinctive and evocative terrace (oh, how I wish Lowry had brought his easel and canvas), are glad that Berwick are still here, glad that football is back. Bonnyrigg supporters stand raucously though peaceably among them, and once again I wonder: where exactly does segregation and acrimony begin, and on what basis is it decided when we fans need dividing from each other and when we don't?

Then, something happens. Berwick score. Berwick, browbeaten and put-upon, hounded and hammered Berwick, score. The cheer is louder than seems possible, as if all home supporters

Night falls over Shielfield Park, Berwick.

suddenly have two voice boxes. All that pain, all that traipsing to the ground and that turning up for nothing but defeat momentarily floats out of their mouths like a lifted curse. We're gonna win the league.

Bonnyrigg score four before half-time. The game ends 3-5. The old, unmovable scoreboard behind a goal that reads "Rangers 0 Visitors 0" seems sarcastic. Offensive, even. Football is wonderful, football is dreadful.

Ninety-four miles away as the gull flies, a few days on in their own maiden fixture, Cove Rangers are ready to flicker and shine. It says something about footballing sympathies that more people know about the Highland League's worst team than its dominant best. Where Fort William are tabloid curios and natural television, the club from south Aberdeen are familiar only through whispers and rumours – oil money this, unmatchable wages that. Upon promotion, supporters of other Highland clubs seemed glad to see them go. Moneybags Cove were their fairy tale villains: rich, arrogant and loathed.

Beyond the rancour are some undeniable truths. This is a slick, well-run and apparently sustainable club. The year-old Balmoral Stadium is commercially maximised and profitably used. This is no new club, a charge that will be hurled at them if they rise through the divisions as some expect. In three years, they will celebrate their centenary. Cove Bay was a village of granite quarries and graft. Such places always need a football team, even if here, residents looked first to Pittodrie.

Today, they tear into Edinburgh City, another recent accession to the Scottish Professional Football League. Sharp and snarling, the home side score five and concede none. Five goals, another diverging parallel with Berwick in which the English side come to grief. Their new life is all cake and ale compared to the crumbs and gruel of Shielfield. And yet... well, you may have guessed where I'd rather be.

Follow the yellow brick road. Shielfield Park, Berwick.

Berwick defend a corner from Bonnyrigg Rose.

The main stand at Shielfield Park, Berwick.

Alan McRae Stan
BALMORAL
BALMORAL OFFSHORE
ACE
ACE
ACE
ACE
ACE

Final preparations ahead of Cove Rangers' inaugural league match against Edinburgh City.

It's all too easy for Cove Rangers as their support celebrate another goal.

Behind the goals at the Cove Rangers-Edinburgh City League Division 2 clash.

In the shadow of the telecommunications towers, Cove Rangers defeat Edinburgh City 5-0 in their first ever league match.

Oor Wullie's chips are BRAW!

Pre-match pints in the sun prior to the first game of the season, and
Cove Rangers' first ever league fixture.

Corner to Cove Rangers at the Balmoral Stadium.

Queuing for the first senior league game at Cove's Balmoral Stadium.

Chapter

Lowland games

The gentle pleasures of Borders football

Sometimes in these still lands, it is hard to imagine a ball being kicked. It seems too strenuous, too disruptive. The Borders are Scotland's gentlest quarters, serene towns and villages of folk who listen first and talk second. The countryside is polite and cushioning, a lie-in instead of an early start.

Here until not so long ago, days jolted along to the clunking noises of textile mills. You can see some of them now in the valley that holds Galashiels in its palm. In bold stone and slate, a number are repurposed. A few are derelict, the forgotten mansions of industrial clout.

Today, the Gala Water which once powered them sloshes onwards as if searching for something to do. It looks like it has taken a wrong turning, or misremembered its course: *have you seen the mill, I'm sure it used to be here...* It rattles away next to us as we walk to the ground, its utterings not unlike those of a crowd in the distance.

To see the football in these parts, one must look beyond the rugby. So it is walking this way to Netherdale, where the pebbledash of Gala RFC comes before the Brutalist majesty of Galashiels Fairydean Rovers FC. Beyond the turnstiles, the players of Gala and Keith do their hopscotch warm-ups and steam rises from the tea hatch. The hatch and café area are new additions, a series of fairy doors for child's play behind the goals too. In every increment it can afford, here is a club devoted to widening its appeal.

Little could improve the bar underneath the stand. It is the ticking heart of Fairydean Rovers. Here, wins are predicted and sorrows drowned. Old pals sit together and beckon over the new. The game matters, but not so much as these segments of the day – nothing staves off lonely winters like laughter and shared jeers as the scores from elsewhere come in. Not that, later on, those scores will linger on the bar's television for long; usually, football coverage makes way, a music radio station is tuned into and turned up, and the rest of the evening becomes pleasantly foggy.

The home side have lost four on the bounce, their visitors nine. Perhaps a cup tie will shake free a win. A Keith supporter tells me a tale of his dad. In 1928, as a boy he had watched Celtic come to town in another cup tie, far from here and now. The Hoops changed clothes and prepared away from the ground before marching through tough northern streets in their full kits. The supporter goes quiet. Marching through his mind are green and white ghosts clacking on cobbles.

The football is urgent. Netherdale's 3G bounce occasionally flummoxes the Keith players, puppies chasing leaves in a breeze. Regardless, they score twice and don't concede. In the Gents' afterwards one man sighs and says to another: "Ach, what else would you do with your Saturdays?" "Exactly," the other replies, "see you next week."

On some other Saturday, we pass more gargling waters in Selkirk and Hawick. It is a soggy afternoon. At Yarrow Park, the goalnets are pinned to the crossbar. There will be no game. Postponement, that

Supporters at Netherdale,
Gala Fairydean Rovers.

dreaded word. The dug-outs are empty, the 'Players and Officials' door is bolted. There may as well be a 'No Ball Games' sign. Birdsong is the only sound. Snow festers on hills beyond the ground, winter reminding all that it is still alive and well. Oh, to watch a game from that shepherd's kop.

A few miles away, Hawick Royal Albert play on, their neighbours, too, the town rugby club. Civil Service Strollers are down from Edinburgh. All-blues versus all-reds, the colours of table football or Subbuteo starter-sets. The turnstile doubles as a programme stall and club shop. Genial Eileen in her Honorary President badge takes our money and sells the club to us. Her enthusing stops only when Royal Albert, embedded at the table's foot, are granted a penalty. It is screwed wide. "Ah just... cannae... believe it," she chokes. Football teams mean the same to those who follow them whatever the venue and scale, wherever you are in the country. Calamitous failings wreck Saturdays from Parkhead to Wick.

Up on the wooden benches of a quietly regal main stand, other supporters can believe what Eileen can't. They have seen it time and again this season. The penalty miss is as inevitable as the five Strollers goals that follow. In the Art Deco directors' box seats, foreheads fall into hands. Robust men question why they bother, and wonder why they were born to love the sphere and not the oval. For a while they think about giving up. They will be back in a fortnight, though; football breeds homing pigeons.

It is best to let matches such as this and places like Albert Park just happen to you. That way are you pleasantly beguiled by the forest that lines the opposite touchline, and enormously comforted by the familiar stock names of Scottish football as they are barked: *DAVEY! STEVIE! WEE MAN! BIG MAN!* Further, you may become engrossed by the varied noises a wet football pitch makes – squelches, paddling, slurps, slaps, gurgles. You may fixate upon a single tear of rain falling from the stand's guttering. You may follow its course as it bounces dangerously close to a coffee mug marked 'TWAT' perched upon the MDF roof of the dugout. You may smile as the Strollers manager offers his gloves to the frozen linesman. You may sigh happily and reflect: what bliss it is to be under football's spell.

At 0-5, the Hawick goalkeeper makes as good a save as I have ever seen. Only the raindrops clap.

The Peter Womersley-designed main stand at Netherdale, Galashiels.

NETHERDALE
the power to play

The Brutalist splendour of the main stand at Netherdale in Galashiels.

Architectural detail, Netherdale, Gala Fairydean Rovers.

20p in. The Womersly designed main stand at Netherdale, Galashiels.

Irene Hutchison,
Honorary President,
Hawick Royal Albert.

Netherdale, home of Gala Fairydean Rovers.

tyres.co.uk
KUMHO TYRES
stle's Tyres
ROVERS FC

Away. Yarrow Park, Selkirk FC.

Raydale Park, Gretna.

The Scottish FA 'office', Netherdale,
Gala Fairydean Rovers.

The clubhouse, Yarrow Park, Selkirk FC.

The club bar, Netherdale, Gala Fairydean Rovers.

The main stand, Ferguson Park,
home of Whitehill Welfare.

Supporters watch Whitehill Welfare
at Ferguson Park, Rosewell.

Supporters (don't) watch Whitehill
Welfare at Ferguson Park, Rosewell.

Overlooked by a hotel, the floodlights are shining by the main stand at Albert Park, Hawick.

TWAT! Albert Park, Hawick.

Chapter

Blaes of glory

Red ash pitches, western Scotland's wound theatres

We play on dust, on tarmac, on grass, on mud, on sand, on rubber. All across the universe, underneath our kicking feet anything will do. Any surface close to solid is good enough. Humans would play football on water if they could. Sometimes *we* choose where to play – the cul-de-sac or scrubland, the back green with its No Ball Games sign or the beach. Goalposts and markings are invented or imagined. Elsewhere, authorities and organisers shoo us onto their facilities, on parks and by playgrounds, or under roofs where rules denounce any ball played above head height. There are painted touchlines and rusty stanchions, changing rooms and vending machines.

On arrival in Scotland, very little can prepare the outsider for his or her first sight of a blaes surface, more commonly known as a 'red ash pitch'. It may stir memories of *Gregory's Girl* – it is on the crimson dust of one such field in Cumbernauld that Dorothy slaloms between multi-coloured cones. Yet that pitch first spotted from train or car is dismissed as an aberration, an eccentricity: surely nowhere else, you think, can they play football on clay the colour of a wet sticking plaster? Then you notice another, and another. From a distance, with dog-dirt and damage impossible to see, they seem, somehow, exotic.

Though blaes stretches across the Central Belt, the epicentre is Glasgow – from above, it must look as though a thousand damp deserts are pushing up and consuming buildings and tarmac. Walk away from Sauchiehall Street in any direction and soon you will see a red blaes pitch. It may languish alone in the middle of a neat suburb of semi-detached homes; it may nestle among half a dozen brother pitches beneath tower blocks, or, at least, where tower blocks once stood. It might be attached to a school, either still in use or pushed to one side by neglect, an embarrassment next to newer facilities, a scruffy uncle sent to the back of the wedding

Red blaes pitch and remains of old railway bridge, Calder Park, Motherwell.

photos. I find these pitches mesmerising. Beautiful, even. This is almost entirely because I never had to play on one.

Before there was red ash, there was black. Municipal pitches were made from coal-mine detritus: goalmouths riddled with lumps and bumps, foul gravel that infiltrated skin like mould on white bread. There were rumours of chrome, cyanide and other industrial waste thrown into the mix. Stories persist of gangrene and even of amputations, young legs lost in the pursuit of joy. Soot: the grim confetti of the disregarded working classes. Let Glasgow Flourish, indeed.

Red blaes came often from West Lothian – it is, essentially, the spoil of the shale oil-mining industry. The cantaloupe-coloured bings we see today from ScotRail or the M8 would once have been used to make football pitches. And, where there's muck, there's brass. Haulage contractors saw the possibilities clearest, shifting blaes by the tonne. Glasgow Corporation and its smaller cousins across the region undertook a mass programme of pitch-building.

Memories of these pitches are synonymous with injury and hardship. As that wonderful sportswriter Hugh MacDonald told the Nutmeg Podcast: "I had post-traumatic stress from playing on red blaes. You had your ash pitches, red or black. Slide tackles were not only allowed, they were mandatory. You would rip your thighs open with surface burns. Someone would come on and scrape it out with a steel brush.

That was when it was good. It could get nasty. It got nasty if there was a game played on it and then overnight it froze over, so you'd have these stalagmites of ash sticking out of the ground like something Indiana Jones had to roll under while he was escaping. These were the pitches that organised football was played on, and it was brutal."

Scuffed knees yawned open and were garnished with this scarlet grit. It clung to every human surface. It still does, in fact; for days after our photo-essay red blaes tour, I was left picking this vibrant clay from my shoes and jeans. No murder mystery author would ever have a suspect run through the stuff – perpetrators could be traced and found within an opening paragraph. "Thirty years on, and I've still got knees like Freddy Krueger's coupon",

Waiting for a match. The perfect red blaes at Calder Park, Motherwell.

wrote one respondent to our enquiries about red blaes.

Games were often played with a Mouldmaster ball, or 'Mouldy'. Inflated to capacity, it could rebound from cold hard blaes with the velocity of a firework. Teeth were lost. The mouldy and its successors would run and run if a shot went wide of goal. Miscued efforts were met with groans from the goalkeeper, now on a faraway chase, and from those forced to stand and wait. Through ice and rain they played on, whether interscholastic or local team games, or informal jostles between all ages and sizes. Always, somehow, did players know whose team they were on. Returning back to lessons or home for tea, torn uniform and ripped tracky bottoms had to be explained; the blaes respected no garment. On a windy day, this surface made for a dust storm. Nature painted players so that they resembled Morphs in trainers. And yet, it is possible to elicit tender memories alongside aching ones from those who played on ash – scorchers from 30 yards, the follies of wonder saves that left human-shaped grooves in the surface for weeks, a terrific bounce that enabled a goal from the halfway line. Memories and shadows, days recalled in a certain shade of red.

In the *Gregory's Girl* territory of Cumbernauld, there are still 27 blaes pitches; Gregory, Dorothy and Susan's school, Abronhill, has been knocked down, but their red ash theatre of wounds remains. Gradually, though, these pitches are disappearing. Some are underused – grass pushes through and seems to ask the question: *why did you never think of me?* Others are built upon or demolished for new surfaces and fresh strategies. Most councils talk of clearing all blaes, but complete obliteration is difficult to imagine, not least amidst gossip including terms like 'undocumented waste'. Few know What Lies Beneath. The preferred surfaces of the day are 3G and 4G. They shine fulgent and ring the tills of councils and football clubs. But how will they look in a quarter-century, and how will we view the materials they are made from? Ingesting their rubber crumb pellets feels far from safe.

Still, we play on. For better or worse, we need to. Where there is ground, there is football. Where there is football, there is escape.

The blaes pitch tucked away between Kent Road and Dover Street in central Glasgow.

The irresistible lure of the red ash - Ashfield Street, Glasgow.

By the Bog Stank, Old Glasgow Road, Cumbernauld.

Past and future. The neglected blaes football pitch and the well-tended kids playpark in central Glasgow.

A miniature red ash pitch in Jordanhill, Glasgow.

Headers and volleys in the midst of the Victorian order of Kelvingrove Park, Glasgow.

Looking over the red ash pitches. Calder Park, Motherwell.

A wheelbarrow sits quietly where once the defensive line stood firm, on the blaes pitches between Maryhill Road and Queen Margaret Drive, Glasgow.

Earmarked to be developed for housing, the blaes pitches between Maryhill Road and Queen Margaret Drive still boast 1,000-year-old goalposts.

The Hopetoun Bing, near Broxburn: a relic of the shale industry and the raw material for red blaes.

Chapter

Under the lights

The magic of floodlit football never fades

It is faint but it is there, a mere clipping of memory. I am sitting on a terrace at Ayresome Park, Middlesbrough, beneath the blood-red crush bar, looking upwards. The game grunts ever onwards, but I do not watch. My eyes face the night sky. I am nine years old and have never seen it looking like this before. It is 8pm, late autumn and all above should be slate-black in this grim march towards winter in north-east England; instead, it glows bright as if God has poked a hole in the sky so that he might watch the match.

Night did not look like this anywhere else. There were hazy satsuma streetlamps and shimmering Christmas decorations, and blinking cinema signs or cosy moonlight – all exciting and comforting, but nothing like four pylons brightening a football ground. Floodlights turned their pocket of town into a travelling circus or a fairground, the centre of attention and the only place to be. They transferred areas that were dingy or unremarkable by day into showbiz venues exuding unlikely glamour, as when an impossibly attractive woman enters a stinking and gloomy pub. Floodlights turned football into something else altogether. It was the same sport with its bawling and huffing, its elation and exasperation, but now it felt somehow inverted or enhanced, as if it had been reimagined by Roald Dahl. Yet here is the greatest part of this sorcery: it still does, and floodlights are still enchanting.

They still glow from afar beckoning us across town or city like the Three Wise Men and their star. They still smother surrounding streets in the pale gold of Easter egg wrapping foil. They still illuminate and dramatise the rain that swarms past them, adding horror-film melodrama absent on a Saturday afternoon. They still hover above the happy tumult in that precious half-hour leading to kick-off,

Ibrox Park under the lights.

shrouding stage lighting on the theatre of programme sellers, ticket queues and old pals worshiping statues. They still blind you when you follow a high clearance, and linger on the backs of your eyelids as you lie awake later, gleeful and frenetic like a kid on candyfloss. They still paint the pitch the colour of a chocolate lime sweet, making grass, somehow, an abstract work worthy of a prize. They still throw shadows on players, who sometimes are pursued and mimicked by a whole quartet of dancing pickpockets. They still change the atmosphere in grandstands and terraces, so that the noises from the seated and the standing are fresher, crisper, more audible now. They still lend the feeling that you, the supporter, are doing something secretive and contraband – while most of the country watches television and yawns towards bed, the fan is wide awake and illuminous. They still leave you enraptured and besotted, so that the next day, when you talk about the game, you follow all your yarns with those magnetic words: 'It was under the lights.'

Floodlights are there for you from Dingwall to Annan. They gleam upon Aberdeen, Ayr and Coatbridge. Their breeds are many: the lustrous and leggy old pylons and egg-yolk globes of Cappielow; the handsome and confident corner landmarks of Palmerston, sure and resolute as sea captains in a storm; the incandescent prize-boards of Pittodrie, which must tempt North Sea mermaids; the roof-joint prongs of Stark's Park, standing to attention and fixated on the pitch; the smart beanpoles of East End Park which radiate like welcome search helicopters; the crooked-necked wonders of Tannadice, keeping a watchful and caring eye... On it goes, through the modern lamps clamped to stand roofs, and the standard-issue poles, not everything beautiful, but all of it useful. Beneath the transfixing rays of the new and the old, happy hearts rumble for floodlit football. Floodlights make children of us all.

The burger van. A warm friend on cold night matches.

Lights above St Mirren Park.

Raydale Park, Gretna.

St Johnstone take on Motherwell under the lights at McDiarmid Park.

MGARRIE & SON
PERTH
TARGETT LANDSCAPING
Garden Design and Construction
INSTANTIMAGE
SIGNS & VEHICLE GRAPHICS
GS Brown
Private Dinners
Meetings
01738 459090
Cairngorm Hotel
sky SPORTS
Ladbrokes Ladbrokes
BINNGROUP

Angles, light and geometry at St Mirren Park.

The inviting lights of Somerset Park, Ayr.

St Mirren Park on a bitterly cold winter's evening.

Chapter

Away days

The glory and dismay of watching your team elsewhere

"Alloa station had never seen such a throng. Men and boys dominated but there was enough feminine colour to complement the black and gold favours worn by almost everyone. The time was just after noon, Saturday 4th March 1939, and the folk, in happy holiday mood, awaited the first of the three special trains to whisk them to Waverley Station in Edinburgh. Not only trains were being filled; service buses were triplicated and special buses were hired; private cars were filled and on the move."
Alloa Official Commemorative Handbook, 1947

You sigh and your shoulders droop. Never again. That *Never* is declared once more behind a chalky cloud fired by your own breath against the bitter and black air. You repeatedly shake your head, as if being interrogated by some unseen ghoul. All that money spent. All the miles crossed by train, car or bus. All of those other things you could have been doing, and instead you were watching a capitulation in Greenock, a rout in Dundee, a hiding in Dingwall, a trouncing in Stranraer. Could even the worst cinema trip, popcorn prices and all, feel half as bad as conceding an injury-time winner? Could even a doleful traipse around a retail park have foisted upon you quite the same gloom as a 3-0 defeat and one shot on goal? When you are there, an away defeat somehow feels thicker, more profound, more scarring, more alienating than its homemade equivalent. It jars. Losing at your place, there is comfort in numbers and routine, in dwelling and wallowing among people and bricks you know well. Losing away, you traipse out into the unfamiliar, you are outnumbered by smiling faces whose joy you resent, you amble past their landmarks and through their streets, an ignored ghost in the wrong house.

Something probably goes awry on the way home: flat tyre, cancelled train, shut pub. The away day festers on Monday and still rankles on Wednesday. Then, on Thursday a whisper niggles: perhaps Peterhead away next week will be a cracker, perhaps you'll put things right at Palmerston, perhaps you'll get something at East End Park, you usually do, or so it feels in the blinkered logic of grief. Saturday morning bends your ear with

The Four in Hand supporters coach, en route to an away match at Ayr United.

talk of places on the coach and a ticket going spare; Saturday afternoon twists your arm with a home victory. You're going. Away again, like nothing could possibly go wrong.

> **"The Kaiser has always been famous for the quality of the language he uses when in his high falutin moods, but the floe of 'flowery' composition which was heard in the vicinity of Tam's Brig on Saturday about one o'clock surpasses anything the deposed Hun head was ever father of. The cause of the fiery outburst was the non-materialisation of a certain means of transport to Kilmarnock, which had been promised to a coterie of rabid football enthusi-asts".**
> *Ayrshire Post, 1918*

We have always gone away. If it wasn't a steam-train coach full of your brethren, it was the merry charabanc. The wild boys of the Brake Clubs even used horse-drawn wagonettes. Flat-capped cyclists travelled too, clunking past ragged-trousered walkers. Folk of the same town and the same team, banded together, representatives, diplomats in knitwear.

From the Brake lads smashing up shops and stoning goalkeepers, to those in a casual state of mind, some have not always had a glorious record. Most have, though. Most of us know – and have always known – that an away day is to be treasured and not wrecked. The plans and the early start, the meeting up and the setting off, the travelling and the arriving. Modern life has all but robbed others of such big days out, such jollies with their rituals, endless refreshments, collections for the driver and 5p poker hands. The hiss of a drinks can being opened or the crinkling of foil are musical notes; the scents of sweet tea or simmering pastry are as fond as Grandma's roast dinner.

The day is peppered with moments and sightings that provoke fleeting solidarity: the scarf draped from the car window, the minibus carrying 15 of 'yours', the nods at motorway services, the snatched prediction chats beneath Departures boards at junction railway stations, singing songs of your club outside someone else's. To enter the ground – and how you are envied if it is your first time here – hop those steps and see hundreds, thousands of

Hibs fan Davie McDiarmid waits for the bus on Edinburgh's Easter Road. While producing this book we learnt that, sadly, Davy passed away during the Covid-19 pandemic.

Chef Matty McNeil, laden down with his home-made pies for the bus trip through to Ayr.

your people transposed to another place hastens the pulse and stings the throat. Here is your legion, infiltrating and invading with its war songs, unified and ready. Some you know from home and nod to, the eye contact twinkly, determined and optimistic. Perhaps nothing will go wrong.

> **"The good people of Peebles must have thought their ancient town invaded as they saw the force, three hundred strong, making its way under a banner, which, by its torn appearance, might have done duty at Flodden, up the station road and across the bridge over the Tweed into the town."**
> *Ayr Observer, 1909*

Today the Hibees go south-west, and to Ayr, portside to seaside. No Brake Club, this: the pies are homemade, the truffles too. *Truffles*. Green and white seems to give a feeling of strength in unity, a shield. A bowling club welcomes the hordes, this jovial army. There is pleasure at thirsts met. At seductive Somerset Park they arrive among thousands of their singsong own. Everything goes right. Hibs win 4-0. They bounce and swagger back to the coach like so many zoo penguins at feeding time.

Those coaches now sound like school trips with no teachers on board. Football is Godly. Life is Wonderful. All across the land, this scene is replicated. There is a reverse image too, incited by defeat. In a losing coach or carriage, passengers stare quietly from the window, their moods heavy and grim. The air is cut only occasionally, by dark sardonic comments and grave claims of relegation and disaster. The gleeful fan and the despondent alike crawl across motorways and railways as evening nuzzles in and darkness falls. Back near their towns and cities, they plot the rest of the evening: a few in the local, maybe chips on the way home.

On Sunday, each traveller has a special kind of tiredness. They are fuzzy, leggy, still partially delirious. In victory and defeat they are comforted by one thing: that they were there, among so many of their own. They belong, home or away.

Waiting for the Four In Hand Supporters Club bus to Ayr United.

Fans gather outside the Somerset Park club shop as kick-off approaches.

Leaving early, Ayr United fans have seen enough.

Finding a different viewpoint from
the old main stand at Somerset Park.

The main stand at Ayr United's Somerset Park on a perfect late autumn day, as the home team take on Hibernian.

EXIT
Record
sunday mail
Ladbrokes

Somerset Park, Ayr. The perfect antidote to the slick and soulless march of modern football.

Hibs go one goal up and the terraces are happy.

Hibs fans on the Somerset Park terracing.

The queue for the burger van as kick-off looms.

The match nears its conclusion as Hibs run out 3-0 winners and The Four in Hand supporters club are happy.

Daily Record
Ladbrokes

The sun sets on the park - and Ayr United, three goals to nil down.

Hibs fans nip out moments after the final whistle blows. A fine result on the road.

After a 3-0 away win, happy Four in Hand supporters head homewards.

Heading home after a grand day out.

Chapter

Gutsy, committed, unflagging

A rich community spirit surrounds Junior football

"It's just a wee bit of weather for Christ's sake. There's nothing wrong with this pitch." The groundsman urges his roller over a corner of the Dunterlie Park turf. A tide of mucky water surges forwards and comes to rest a few centimetres beyond the touchline. "We want a game," he continues, eyes fixed on the roller, voice croaking at the idea of an empty afternoon. As all football watchers know, the postponed match pillages the day of its purpose. It presses Pause. In rain is there purgatory.

The Barrhead skies have blubbered since yesterday. Rain raps on the main stand roof like a loan shark's knuckle on a tower-block door. It worries guttering and falls in capsules from the goal nets. Still, no supporter brings an umbrella. Volunteers aged schoolboy to pensioner graft on, pushing slurping torrents of water from the pitch and pocking it with pitchforks. They want their game.

At 1pm, an hour before kick-off, there is a pitch inspection. Arthurlie versus Glenafton Athletic is on. "A big call" says to me the Glenafton goalkeeping coach. The home blue and whites and the away red and whites traipse onto the pitch to warm up. Their studded steps make a slapping noise. Many shake their heads but within minutes are dedicating their all to running drills. When you play Juniors, you play because you bloody well love football. Copious rain and pitches resembling Saxon wrestling pits are mere backdrops.

Just before 2pm, the match is called off. Purgatory is here. They have not got their game.

The Ayrshire climate wants a game, though. Above coal pit hills that now rest in angry peace, there are clear skies, sharp air and a determined egg yolk sun. It hangs low, meaning many a supporter's arm will be raised to visor position. Like umbrellas, baseball caps and Junior Football don't mix. This is bobble-hat football.

Auchinleck is a long village of fetching crimson stone, Cumnock a spacious town of winding river and streets. Neighbours but far from neighbourly when playing one another, both are underpinned by long memories of footballing glory, of full employment and powering Britain, of solid politics and some witch in London picking a fight. Much is gone but football rages on, unperturbed, an unsnuffable candle.

In Auchinleck, nursery rhymes are no longer recited, they've been replaced by Talbot mantras of prowess: champions four years in a row, 11 stars floating on the crest for 11 Junior Cup wins. When they reap silverware, the streets are paved with black and gold. The pit village without a pit comes together just as it did in '84.

Hundreds have gathered today for the visit of Largs Thistle. From Coal Road you hear them, satisfied claps and throaty cries goading on "The Bot". Such a crisp January afternoon makes the referee's whistle shriller. These being the last embers of sunlight – few Junior grounds have floodlights – both teams' colours take on a hazy appearance, as if you are watching a 'dream' sequence in a children's television show. A sign boasts that Auchinleck is the home of Red Kola. One behind-goal terrace is hemmed in by neat miners' housing, each home having a football ground at the end of the garden, and the other by a bustling social club, that unflagging mainstay of Juniors life.

On the pitch, the football is hurried and urgent, full of thunder and bluster, sturdy tackles and cunning wingers. "We need to up the tempo, this is fucking shite," barks a Talbot full-back, to my surprise.

At Cumnock, too, they are playing the kind of gutsy, committed and flawed football too often absent from the error-petrified league game. There is nothing cagey here, no protection rackets or playing for a point. We are invited "upstairs" for a cup of tea with Heather, one of those hidden many who truly make these clubs and this game tick. With two or three others, we watch the game from behind an upstairs window in a room clad with sepia images of 'Nock' glory days. "Over there, where the Beith fans are now, that was a bing. Folk used to stand on there to watch the match," an old man tells me. "I bloody love this club. It's special. Rooted in the community," he continues, beating hard syllables on the floor with his walking stick.

The Nock are 2-1 down and battering at Beith in search of equality. The old man speaks again. "We've had some players here down the years, I tell you." Cumnock equalise. He roars, arms aloft. Another man hands me a book, *The Juniors: The Story of Cumnock Juniors Football Club*. "There you are, son, a wee present for taking the time to come here." Me and the old man flick through the book. He stops at a page of black and white photographs and points at a portrait shot of a player captioned 'Townhead Park fifties idol, the lightning fast powerhouse that was Mick Philips.' He looks me in the eye. "There I am," he says.

Nock Nosh at Townhead Park, Cumnock

TOWNHEAD COMMUNITY SPORTS HUB
NOCK NOSH
SNACK BAR
Soup of the Day
Lentil Soup
£1.00

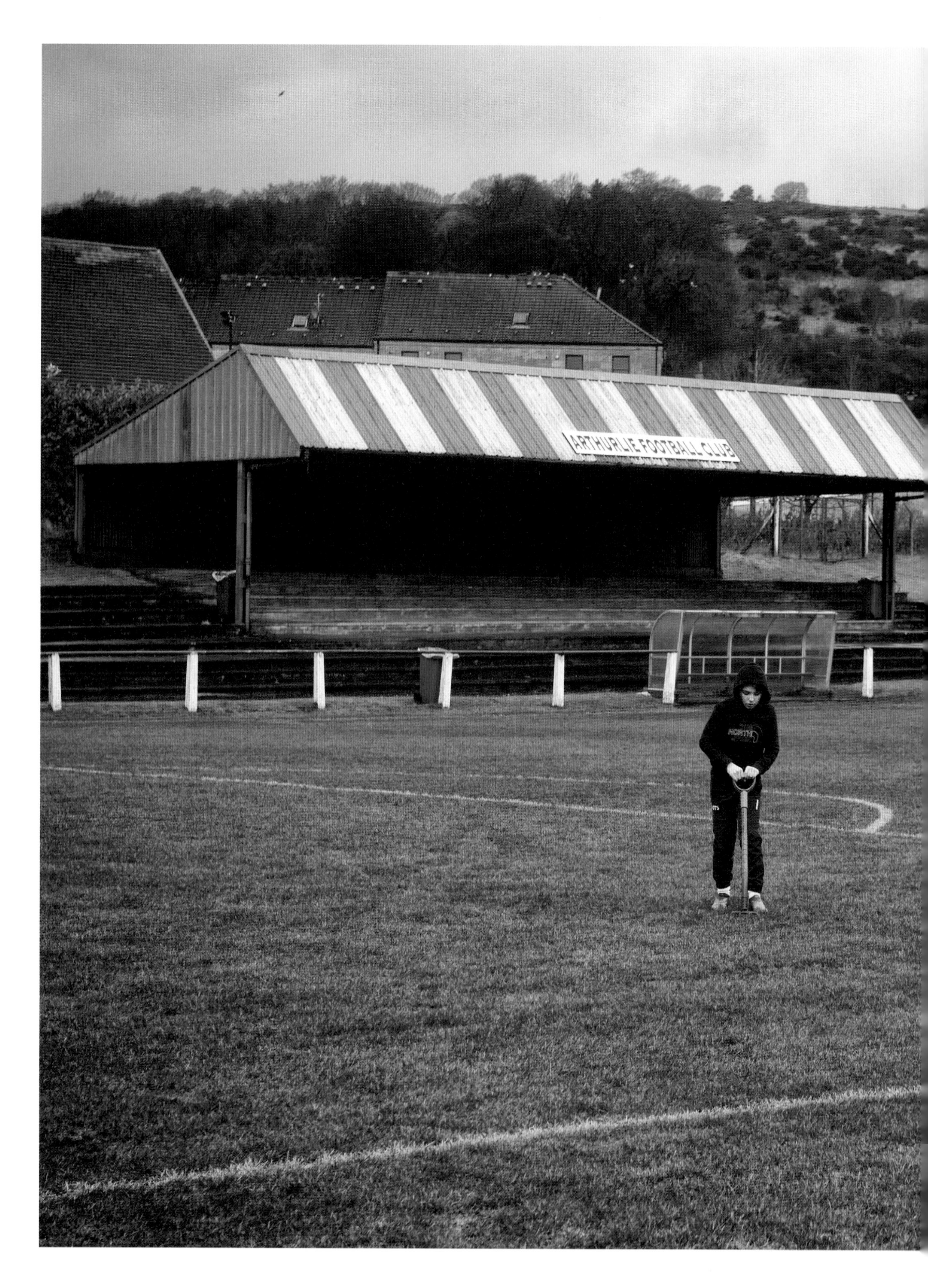
ARTHURLIE FOOTBALL CLUB

Dunterlie Park, Arthurlie FC. Forking the pitch to try and get the surface ready for the afternoon match.

Arthurlie club officials desperately trying to remove water from the pitch, before their match against Glenafton Athletic.

adidas

Auchinleck Talbot fans watch from the stand.

All smiles as Auchinleck Talbot host Largs at Beechwood Park.

No entry as the match between Arthurlie and Glenafton at Dunterlie Park is called off.

The Beith drummer, during the Cumnock v Beith match.

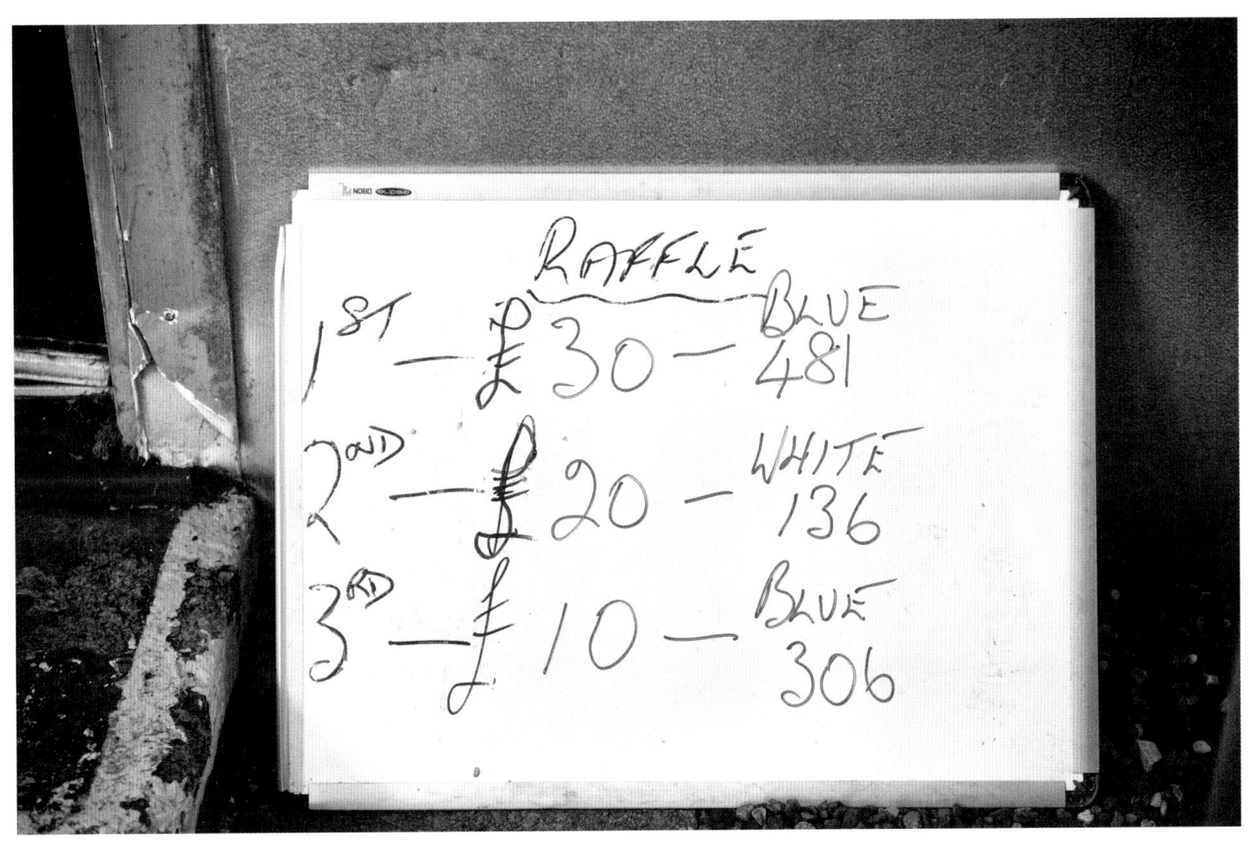

The raffle prizes, Auchinleck Talbot.

Looking on as Cumnock are held to a 2-2 draw by Beith.

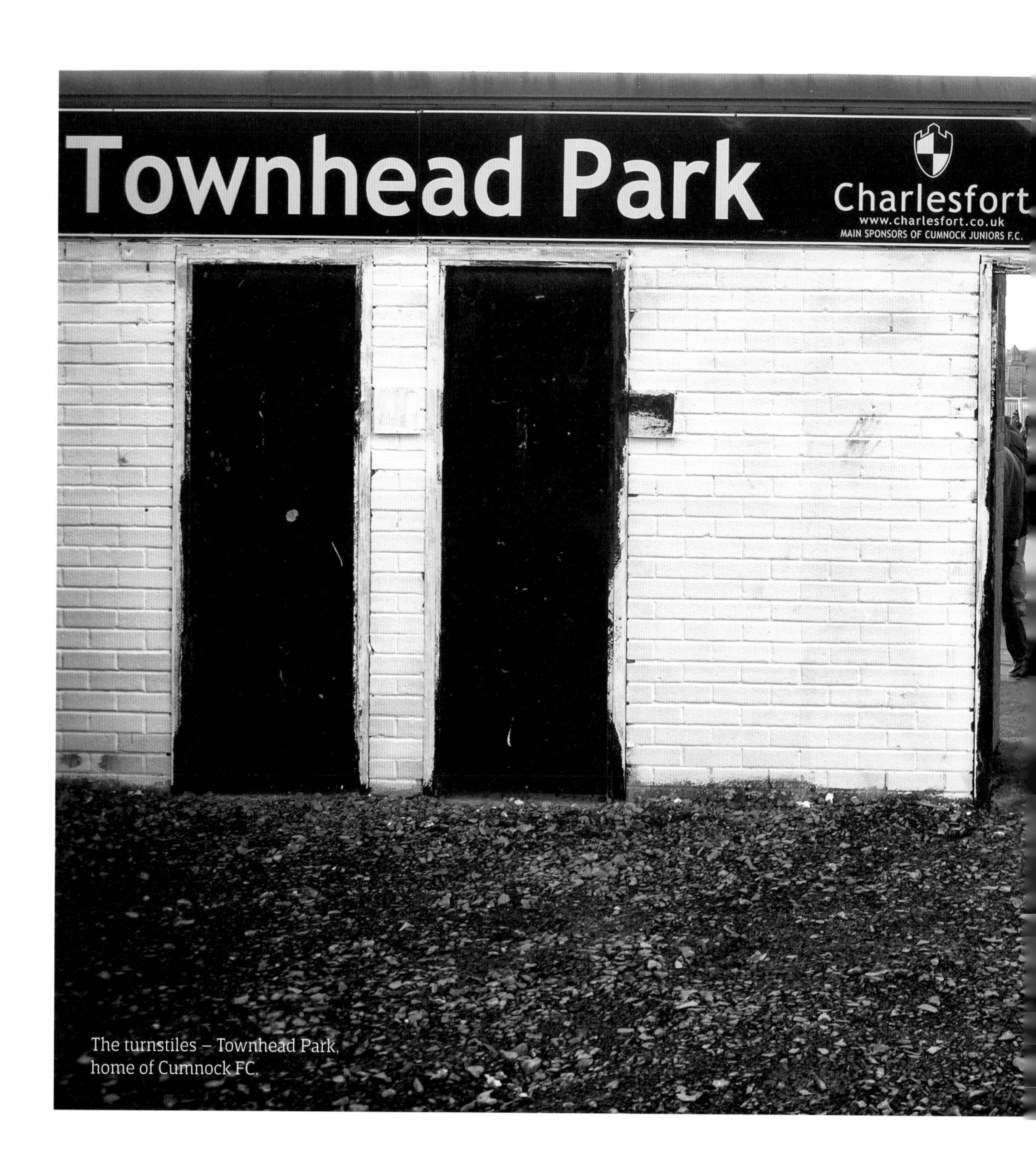

The turnstiles – Townhead Park, home of Cumnock FC.

Checking the scores or making plans for later? Auchinleck Talbot v Largs.

Beechwood Park, Auchinleck.

Snack bar, Auchinleck Talbot.

Beechwood Park, Auchinleck.

Ex-Cumnock player Mick Phillips and club secretary George Morton look on from the Club Tea Room as Cumnock host Beith.

VAUXHALL

Chapter

Ghost homes

Vanished grounds, those lost opera houses of the working class

Late autumn suits Cathkin Park, once home to Third Lanark FC. Leaves the colours of cheese on toast and lovingly polished brown shoes settle on the terraces and gild the melancholy of the place. This old ground is always dying but never dead. No Glasgow Southside soul would let that happen. Every few years, still, there are new plans to wake the old girl and let her live a little.

To walk up and down the three remaining sides of Cathkin is like inhabiting some old man's dream. This is where I stood, he tells you, and that's where all the wee laddies were, down at the front on lemonade crates. He still sees players ducking and weaving in Thirds' scarlet shirts, still hears the wails of derision and the hollers of glory.

Much of the terracing is sheltered by trees planted since the ground was discarded. The matter which falls from them adds mossy liver spots. There are recent empty cans and bottles of lager and Buckfast, echoing those once dropped on matchdays. This litter also reminds the visitor that people still come here – to drink, to jog, to walk the dog, sometimes even to play on the pitch, still marked like the faint outlines of a blocked-off doorway. Old men, now awoken, come too. They stand in their old spot, think, laugh and weep.

Those leaves that still cling to trees sway in the morning bluster. They murmur enough to demonstrate how noise must have swelled across this amphitheatre. There were 45,000 here for a game against Rangers in 1954. By then, Third Lanark were over 80 years old.

In 1889, Thirds beat Celtic 3-0 in the Scottish Cup Final. Players had trudged and kicked in ankle-deep snow, and thrown snowballs at one another. Celtic protested that the result shouldn't stand. Third Lanark won the replay 2-1. A few years on, in 1904, they won the league under manager Frank Heaven. A year later, though only in his thirties, Heaven passed on, we hope to a place matching his name.

Those were the halcyon Saturdays. 1925 reaped relegation, and then decades of bobbing between the divisions merrily enough. In the 1960/61 season, Third Lanark of Cathkin Park were Glasgow football's finest showbiz act, scoring 100 goals and finishing third in Division One. Their swashbuckling centre-forward Alex Harley netted 42 of them.

Enter Bill Hiddleston as chairman, and a crusade of asset-stripping. In these parts,

A reminder that once this supermarket carpark was Brockville Park, the home of Falkirk FC.

they presumed the businessman was letting the club crumble so that houses could be built on Cathkin – this remains a desirable, peaceful locale.

Harley was sold to Manchester City, flourished there, but died at 33. Hiddleston's penny-pinching would have been the stuff of an Ealing comedy, had not a heinous end seemed so inevitable: old footballs painted to look new and leaving marks on footballers' foreheads; players told to hide barroom fruit machines when the taxman called; weekly wages paid in turnstile coins; training conducted in the dark to save on utility bills.

Thirds finished the 1964/65 season at Division One's foot. They had won seven points from 34 games. Soon, the Cathkin terraces were a lonesome place to be. Attendances fell into the hundreds. Hiddleston's tenure was bitter, heart-breaking; Third Lanark supporters were watching their club slowly die, helpless onlookers as a family member perished on the operating table.

The last game at Cathkin took place on 25 April 1967, a 3-3 draw with Queen of the South. Thirds were liquidated in June. 1967, 1967... that golden year for Scottish football. Not here. Here it was a black year. A Trade Inquiry found Hiddleston responsible for gross corruption, and recommended police action. Hiddleston died suddenly of a heart attack in November that same year. Cathkin survived to grow old and weary, the sacred home of a few thousand ghosts.

Two miles away in Rutherglen, there is still weekend sport at the Shawfield ground. On Friday and Saturday evenings, greyhounds circle grass once graced by Tommy Ring, Harry Haddock and many another Clyde FC artisan footballers. It may seem a modern occupancy, but greyhounds have raced here since 1932. In the hungry thirties, dog money often kept Clyde afloat.

Shawfield's surroundings are sparse. There are signs of life on some of the spaces around the ground – housing and offices being built, placards declaring new beginnings – but vast gaps speak of

This entrance to the Royal Gymnasium Ground in the heart of Edinburgh's New Town is all that remains of the home of St Bernard's FC.

bulldozing. When surrounding tenements were cleared, so too were many Clyde supporters – and future Clyde supporters who just didn't know it yet. Shawfield is hemmed in and shrieked at by busy roads on each side. It seems to be squeezing in its shoulders like a burglar hiding behind curtains. Perhaps this way no one will notice it, and it will never face the wrecking ball unlike its neighbouring dwellings.

Were it not here, the Bully Wee would have little connection with a charming past. This is the place where Mattha Gemmell went from physiotherapist to coach to manager in 1909, and didn't leave until 1945. If Shawfield bricks harbour a ghost, it is surely he.

In the early 1910s, his Clyde side was one of the best in the land: 48,000 saw them beat Rangers here and go on to lose the Scottish Cup Final against Celtic. In 1939, they finally won the thing. "For the semi-final and final rounds we stayed in Troon," said goalkeeper Jock Brown. "We trained on the sands and played pontoon till 3am." There were 94,000 people at Hampden as the Bully Wee defeated Motherwell 4-0. "Ma boys did it! They did it!" a jubilantly dazed Gemmell repeated over and over as Shawfield danced to the tune of champagne corks.

By the time those Shawfield lads like Haddock and Ring won the cup again in 1955 and 1958, Gemmell had retired. On each occasion, the team bus stopped and its passengers waved the trophy to a tenement window at 236 Main Street, Bridgeton. In return, long-term resident Mattha Gemmell flourished his Clyde-white handkerchief.

Those were the days. Now, Bully Wee followers have to be old to remember them. They remember, more, ground-sharing at Partick and Hamilton, and finally moving to a home of sorts in Cumbernauld.

At least they still had a club. Falkirk too. Their Brockville ground is commemorated outside the Morrisons supermarket that replaced it. A Mancunian turnstile in ornate iron is poignant and starkly beautiful, like spotting a swan among seagulls. It feels, though, as if the saddest gesture of all is the way that Brockville, like so many other grounds, could not be redeveloped. Here was a town-centre home with tight terraces and dome-topped crush barriers. It brimmed with charisma; in one corner was a small window belonging to a house on Watson Street, from which occupants could watch the game. It was a loud and intimidating theatre set among the streets from which Falkirk fans came. So close was Brockville to Falkirk Grahamston station, it was said that a ball launched over the Hope Street End had once landed in a passing freight truck and travelled 43 miles north to Perth. Now, the Bairns play among roads and spaces, one end absent as if they bought the stadium in a box and found that a piece was missing.

In the future, it is likely that the sacking of grounds will be widely regretted. The 1990s and first two decades of 21st-century stadium development will be ruefully viewed as 1960s and 1970s urban demolition and town planning are now. Why, it may be asked, could old architecture and charm not be included in modern, safe redesigns, instead of ripping it all to shreds and beginning again with artless soccer domes? Original gems could have been incorporated into plans, as happens now with theatres, libraries and museums in historic centres. Few authorities or institutions cared, though, about the plight of old grounds, those lost opera houses of the working class.

In Edinburgh, St Bernard's Gymnasium Ground was situated at the foot of Scotland Street, possibly the least working-class area this side of the Maldives. What remains is a fence and gate, which once led into the back of the main stand. On the steps opposite, at 15 Royal Crescent, a shell-shocked World War One veteran named Willie would sit. Every day, he would ask those walking by: "Is there a game on?"

"Not today, Willie," was the usual reply, "not today."

Behind the goals. The old west terracing at Cathkin Park.

Behind the billboard lies the old entrance to Shawfield, home of Clyde FC for almost a century.

LD
SHAWFIELD DR
primesight
1015 02
uites
We're now on
Facebook
Why buy an ordinary
gift when your mum
is anything but?
ebay
Fill Your Cart
With Colour

All that remains of Brockville, once home to Falkirk FC, is a turnstile in a supermarket carpark.

Cathkin Park corners.

Tinto Park in Glasgow, the now demolished home of Benburb FC

A lone supporter watches from overgrown terracing as Benburb play their last

Chapter

Beer and sympathy

The social clubs of football are charming netherworlds

There was a simple pattern to the nights when my dad was in charge. First, a plate of his homemade chips, delightful splinters of potato crackling. Then, a familiar and gentle instruction: "You choose a video while I wash the pots."

Our VHS collection took up the bottom trunk of an old chest of drawers. It only ever opened reluctantly and stuffily, as if it thought it should be storing something more vintage and stately than plastic blocks. Yet Dad and I revered this drawer. Its contents could take us to Ayresome Park or Elland Road and acquaint us with Pelé or Johan Cruyff. There was the odd official club video or BBC compilation tape, but most of our viewing was recorded from the telly, 'BORO v BOLTON W' scribbled over *Howard's Way* or 'Mum's tape'. Despite all of this, and despite our shared football addiction, the video I often selected contained neither goals culled from local news bulletins nor documentaries narrated by Barry Davies.

'Golden Gordon' was an episode of *Ripping Yarns*, a comedy series written by Terry Jones and Michael Palin. In it, Palin plays Gordon Ottershaw, a heartbreakingly fanatical and farcically loyal supporter of Barnstoneworth United, quite comfortably the worst team in West Yorkshire. My general obsession with Ottershaw and Barnstoneworth lasts to this day (my dad and I have a brick inscribed outside the Riverside Stadium. It says nothing about Middlesbrough FC, but instead carries a quote from 'Golden Gordon'). It was, though, a specific location in the programme that fixated me as a child: The Barnstoneworth United Social Club.

After another heavy defeat, Gordon declares to his wife that he is going "somewhere to cheer myself up". We cut to an austere, brown and cream room

3-1 down at half-time, at home. Long faces in the Cumbernauld United Social Club.

containing no other drinkers, and a dour, distracted barman named Cyril. There is, on the wall, a mahogany board displaying United's achievements. Ottershaw will later kick it so that it splits perfectly into two parts. It is here too, that to the devastation of Gordon, the chairman will announce the closure of Barnstoneworth United, and the selling of its beloved Sewage Works Ground to the Arthur Foggen Scrap Company.

That a football club might have its own sociable quarters thrilled me as a child. It meant that a team was alive seven days a week, that supporters had somewhere to go, somewhere to indulge in that one topic that truly mattered, the one shut down by so many disinterested others: their team. Sadly, I would have to wait thirty-odd years before finding anywhere that embodied this idea; until Scotland I was never happy.

XMAS SHOW – HOT BUFFET reads the bright and busy noticeboard at the Linlithgow Rose Social Club, then ANGELA MINTY AND MICKEE BLITZ (GLAM ROCK TRIBUTE). Posters and signs are important in social clubs. There are advertisements for Race Nights, Vocal Entertainers, Fantastic Female Vocal Artistes, Sensational Female Vocal Entertainers and Terrific Female Vocal Entertainment From The North East. There are reminders that "Membership can now be uplifted and paid for" in that old-man handwritten font that mixes upper and lower case, and is underscored with a wavy red line. All patrons are asked to "Please Use Trays" when carrying drinks from bar to table.

These places are never as joyless as the Barnstoneworth United Social Club, and closer, in fact, to another televisual heaven from northern England – Brian Potter's Phoenix Club. It is what they represent that takes me back to that

The Cumbernauld United Social Club, at Guy's Meadow.

old video, as if I am not standing in Cambuslang or Whitburn, but reeled inside the tape.

They are, as I'd dreamed, adjuncts of the football club, dwellings that turn them into seven-day outfits, extras and bonuses that enrich and thicken, lounges for those who see their team as a relative. In social clubs, customers share the same worries and aspirations, and are holding conversations about calf strains and equalisers that are unpalatable elsewhere. No one ever shouts and there is never silence – just chatter, hubbub, contentment.

As in Barnstoneworth, honours boards jostle for wall space. They have the dark resonance of war memorials and the celebratory pomp of graduation ceremonies. There is usually a cabinet offering trophies tall or wide, tatty or gleaming. Club pennants line walls, the bunting at the fete, and recall the visits of tropical teams from Italy and Humberside. Usually, there is a television on a bracket or a shelf, silently bringing scores from games in other towns or episodes of *Pointless*.

The cast in this video is familiar, universal. Committee men in grey trousers and blue blazers hover, taking pride and straightening picture frames, the unheralded volunteer regiment nudging football on. Who will do this when they stop? There is a doorman with a margarine tub or charity collection pot for the takings of 50p guests. Someone with no known surname called Davie or Yvonne runs the bar, and Jack and Victor pals cue up their own jokes to begrudgingly fond laughter. In three of the clubs we visit, we're told with a wink that we can take photos "as long as you're no' the DSS". And every now and then when I visit these places, I see lone, intense figures in club hats and scarves staring at old team photos. Always, I text my dad: "Ottershaw found, alive and well."

F.C.
EVERTON
SOUTHAMPTON
NEWCASTLE
SUNDERLAND
BURNLEY
LEEDS
BRISTOL CITY
BLACKBURN
ROCHDALE
CHESTER F'D
BRADFORD
BURY
ABERDEEN
HEARTS
KILMARNOCK
ALLOA
FORFAR
BRECHIN
EAST FIFE

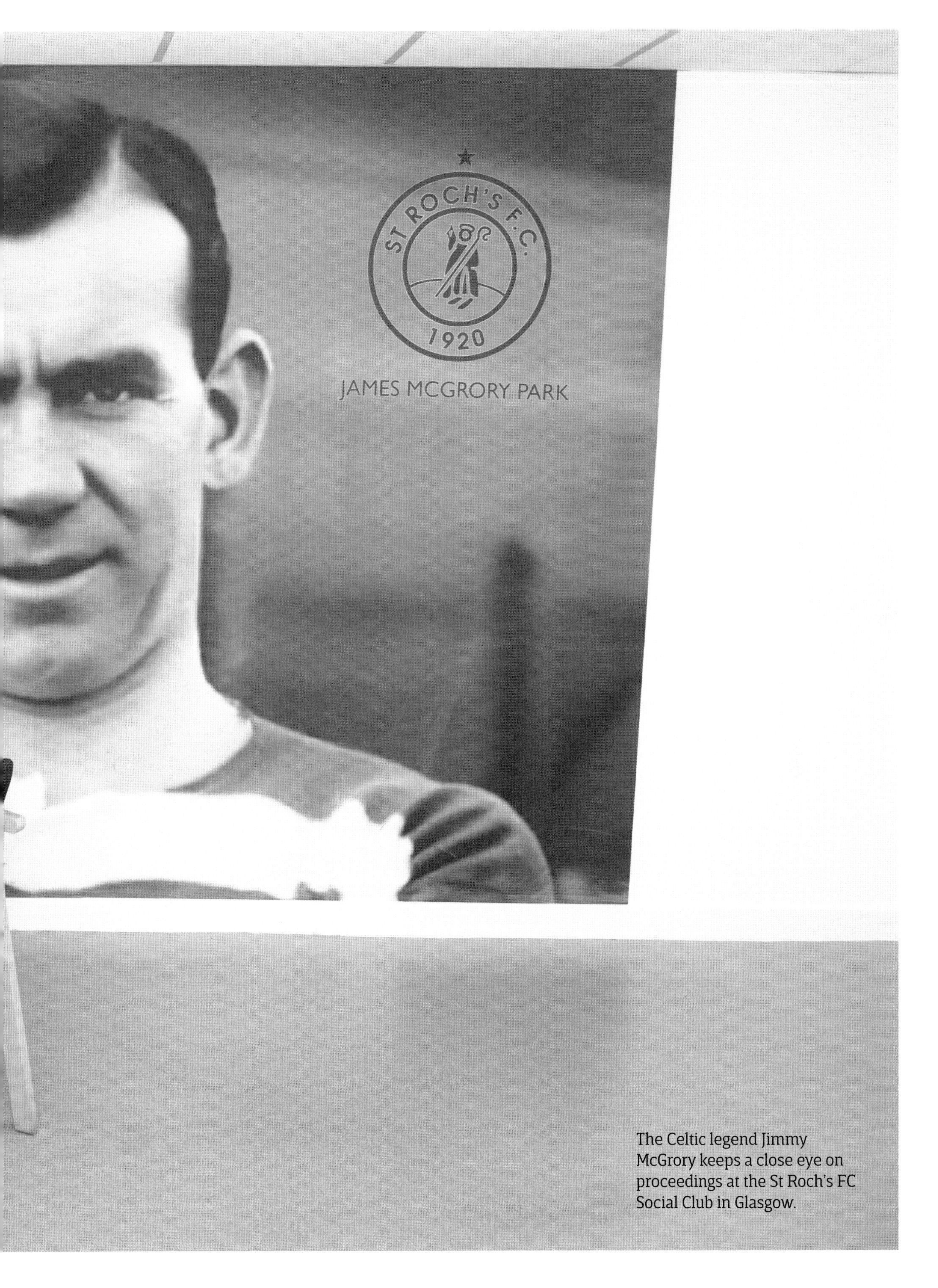

The Celtic legend Jimmy McGrory keeps a close eye on proceedings at the St Roch's FC Social Club in Glasgow.

Time for home – Whitburn Juniors Social Club.

sky SPORTS
HERE
NOTICE
The management cannot
Karma
Indian Cuisine
01501 744024
FIRE EXIT
KEEP CLEAR
CCTV
CCTV

All smiles after a home win at Whitburn Juniors Social Club.

Post-match drinks in the Cambuslang Rangers FC social club.

Happy days at the Hibernian Football Supporters Club.

The half-time rolls are uneaten at the Whitburn Juniors FC Social Club.

Trays must be used at all times, thank you, in the Linlithgow Rose FC Social Club.

Pre-match pint in the Linlithgow Rose FC Social Club.

Come and see Neil Diamond and Elvis Presley at the Linlithgow Rose FC Social Club.

The Lewis & Harris Rangers Supporters Club in Stornoway.

Chapter
10

First time I saw you

The sighting of a new football ground is blissful

You wake and for a few seconds think it is one of those other mornings. The dreary 345-or-so in a year when you're not going to a match. It takes a few seconds to remember what day this is. Who you are, even, especially if Friday night was good. If there was a Friday, though, then this is Saturday. If this is Saturday, the right kind of Saturday, then it is sacred. A day of worship. It is even richer if your pilgrimage will take you somewhere new. To walk around a rosy corner and see a football ground for the first time is bliss.

Happy as you are, there is no leap from bed. You lie there for a few minutes, thinking about the day ahead – even the smiling sun sometimes rises groggily. You think about the travel, the timings, the things that can go wrong, the walk to the ground, and whether there will be a useful pub on the way. Too much thought, however, can spoil this day's finest quality: the unbridled thrill of the new.

Public transport, preferably train, is the best way to arrive in a football territory you do not know. Travelling by car brings too much distracting frustration and conversation, indulgence in which leaves you less able to look out of the window. The broad panes of bus or train open our senses to the different, the meaningful and the new. They widen our eyes, readying them for later spectacles: that first glance around the corner; seeing this particular green for the first time; the game itself.

You drift towards locals in home colours then stalk them loosely like a shambolic private detective. Up pops a pub to fall into. A quick pint, two if you're good, and then off. The last sup is gulped and the glass landed with a thud. To the ground, those beers having polished your senses further and tuned heartstrings. You are ready to take it all in.

The rhythms of matchday are the same, the lyrics altered. The many are on the march, just as happens at home. In hope they stride, here, there and everywhere. But vive la différence – in this foreign land, the shirt colours that seep from beneath jackets and over jeans are blue to your red. Accents drop different sounds and rise where yours sinks. Heroes have different names.

Everywhere, the streets you walk down seem to be lined with ambivalent residents who don't even care that they live near a ground. You rarely see anyone looking out of the window, spectating the parade. Blinds are down, curtains drawn; ye gods, what sacrilege! The hollers of programme-hawkers seem to quicken the pace like church bells hurrying tardy parishioners.

And then you turn the corner, and it is there.

The old ones are the best ones: a slither of ground squatting at the end of a long tenement row; a main stand shrouding a neat estate of inter-war semi-detached houses; the away end panorama blocked by a church of the other kind; a beautiful, scraggy home of football set by industrial scrubland. The first sight of an urban ground is obscured or distracted, making it more tantalising. It has context. The out-of-town ground makes it too easy, offers kisses on the first date.

Look at Firhill, like a Spanish cigarette factory. Look at Ochilview, like an island chapel with the roof blown off. Look at Stark's Park, like a secret naval war machine. Look at Easter Road, a robot ready to unfold and eat Leith. Behold the raw museum loveliness of Dens Park and the bold handshake of a Pittodrie welcome (and what lout would demolish either?)

What corners they are to turn, your visit stacked with a double joy: that rush of a first glimpse, and then these grounds' own unique beauty. In their company, a normal streetscape becomes treasured and surreal. A street's name has so much more meaning. They enrich the tarmac as nothing else can.

Why the locations of football grounds were chosen, we may never know. Who scouted the sites that would be consecrated? What were the criteria? How long did it take for these corners to become hallowed? Thinking from above, it is possible to picture some godly architect dropping terraces upon the righteous.

But to ponder too much is to stifle the tingle. You can over think infatuation. It is emotion that counts most, the way goose bumps can still be enticed after years of football. These grounds may not be yours, but there is a flirt in all of us.

The rolling fields of the Angus countryside break gently against the back of Station Park, Forfar.

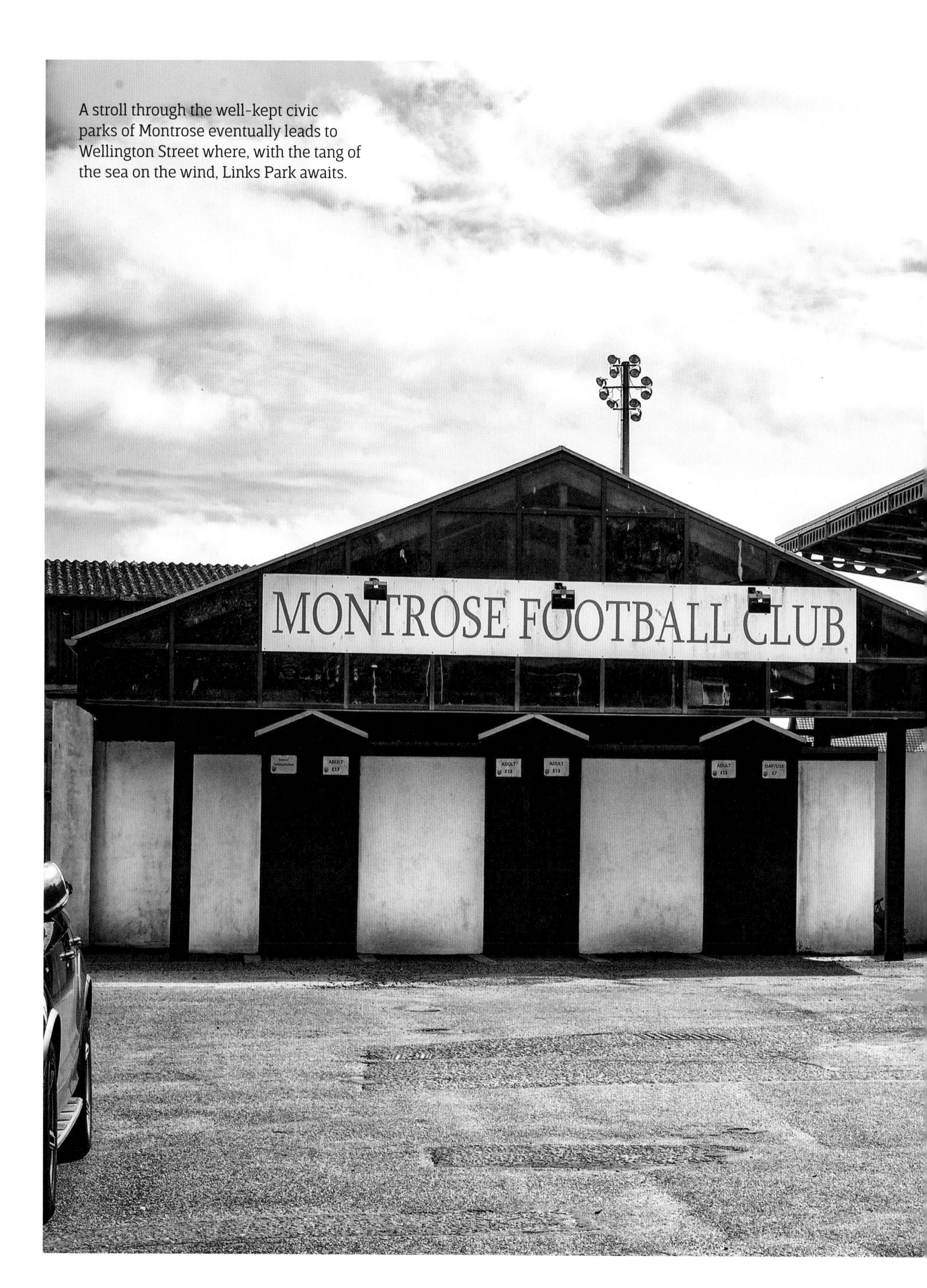

A stroll through the well-kept civic parks of Montrose eventually leads to Wellington Street where, with the tang of the sea on the wind, Links Park awaits.

18-28
CLIO

Dundee FC's Dens Park still shows the ghost of the old earth banking that once formed the structure of so many football grounds.

Tucked away behind new shops, 1930s terraced housing and a golf course lies the colourful façade of Stenhousemuir's Ochilview Park.

The steep approach to Stark's Park, Kirkaldy, one of the finest old grounds in the country.

A narrow gap between a church and Gorgie tenements reveals reveals the Gorgie Stand, forming the southern edge of Hearts' Tynecastle Stadium.

A walk through old sandstone and brick warehouses leads to Tannadice, and the stand named after Dundee United legend, Jim McLean.

Tucked away down a quiet Brechin road, with Victorian villas lining the route, Glebe Park, complete with its hedge, comes box-like into view.

The long walk down the Merkland Road, often in the face of a biting North Sea wind, ends in the chunky granite entrance to Pittodrie.

The old Maryhill tenements that once focused the eye on Partick Thistle's Firhill home may have gone, but the approach up Springbank Street is like taking a walk back in time to a more elegant age.

Chapter
11

The Sunday morning alarm crew

Park football is a messy community, but a wonderful one

Sunday morning. Half-swigged lagers in filched pint glasses rest on walls, marooned nocturnal remnants. A church bell rings tinny, tired and miserable. Parishioners trot to the door in search of answers. Behind drawn blinds, some have arisen earlier than they would like, but many sleep. Old ladies are up and out for rolls and papers, all "How's your Gordon getting on in hospital?" and "Did you hear about Barbara's fall?" This is a gloopy, dozy hour that they share. Every week from summer to spring, their tranquil community is joined by an unlikely huddle: tracksuit-and-holdall men gathering in car parks.

That they do is a laudable feat of obsession and almost eccentric commitment. Very little can stop them turning up to play despite a torrent of reasons not to: the horror of a phone alarm screeching in the bedside dark; the stiff cold that enters toes through the bathroom floor and by mid-morning kick-off calcifies noses; the hours of family time and obligation traded away; the thrashings and the chances of GBH. Some even stay sober on Saturday nights.

Yet look at them on any backwater hovel of a pitch and you will see exactly why they bother. Out there, they are free, in the moment, lost to the chase, gone to the game, kicking and dreaming – even happy, sometimes. If you can find anything that makes you act like that, makes you feel 11 years old again, here is all I know: you hold on to it. You close the front door, you rub your hands together, pick up your boot bag, and you turn up and play.

The first time we try to find them, we see nothing but damp empty spaces. It is a morning of blanket postponements. By fields in all corners of Scotland, men stand shaking their heads and muttering variations of "we used to play in much worse than this" and "bloody health and safety". Referees lie in.

Postponement creates an alternate universe – an uninhabited shadow world where colour and life were scheduled to exist from 10.30 a.m. Net hooks go hungry; crossbars resemble empty curtain rails in an abandoned house. They are upholstered by a hundred stripy flecks of sticky tape, dishevelled bunting from all those weeks

Leaf-clearing duty on Leith Links.

when the football pageant was in town. There are still thimble potholes, the scars of boot studs. Seagulls, and not hollering full-backs, are heard. Stagnant puddles have settled in the centre-circle. It is almost eerie on this abandoned pitch – stare into the rainwater long enough and you might see images of games and scraps gone by.

Seven days later, the skies are settled and this netherworld has been overcome. We hear football before we see it. A referee's shrill whistle and the barking of men. Between us and the pitches is a row of flats, so that the sound is muffled and contorted like that of parents arguing in another room.

Closer to the din, it is possible to decipher sweet and familiar words and phrases, each one an entry in the glossary of park football – "put a name on it!", "Channels!", "Second ball!", "Close him down!", "Square it", "Man on" and "Keeper's!" And on every pitch there are players called "Stevie" and "Wee Man". *Down the line, Stevie...*

There are nets now, some in their team's colours. Those colours are often like the incoherent and unidentifiable kits adorning birthday cards given by 1980s grandmas – a team in After Eight-box green shirts versus one in Uruguayan light blue. Breeze swells to gale and corner flags cower. One slides to the middle of its pole so that it looks like a tutu.

A goalkeeper's towel is blown from its perch in the side-netting. He rehangs it and indulges in two clangs of each boot against the upright, the custodian's equivalent of a maddened bull pawing the ring floor before charging. Perhaps his anger is the consequence of years spent chasing wayward shots as they reel away into the dark edges of parks across the land. He is soon withdrawing, though, caught too far from his box as a forward moves in on goal. The goalkeeper moves backwards like a cat retreating behind an opening door. His opponent, a gangly number 9 with the volatile edge of a felon on the run, pushes the ball beneath him and into the goal. It goes straight through the net's foot and nests in bracken. An extra tent peg is summoned to avoid a repeat incident.

By the side of each pitch is a familiar gaggle of people. There are men in the same official club jumpers and jackets, men who should know better. Some

One man and his dog watching
the football in the park.

even have their initials printed in the chest area. "If you don't want to run around, don't fucking well turn up" is the encouraging cry from one coach. Next to them are always a few shivering substitutes, rolling their feet over footballs, absent-mindedly canoodling and caressing them, and telling lies about Friday night conquests.

There are, too, casual followers of the team, or rather, casual followers of individual relatives in the team, carefully moving around sideline detritus such as discarded energy drink bottles and fluorescent bibs, the spoils of Sunday warm-ups. All who watch are united in their reactions – fiery encouragement when one of their lads Geronimos into a tackle, warm cheers when a goal is plundered, heartfelt winces when a ball pelts into a delicate area with the force of an aggressive masseur's slap.

Adjacent to all of this, or sometimes on their own dedicated fields, the next generation of Sunday morning pilgrims to the mud play. Many show endeavour and harbour dreams of something more. Some stare vacantly at autumnal trees with thoughts of warm indoors and Xbox time never far away. Here do managers imagine themselves to be Napoleons with tactics magnets. Actually, in their cries of "Spin him" and their hectoring of young referees, they are more like the town-centre soapbox preachers that people cross the street to ignore.

Concentrating on such things is churlish. This football is not about what occurs on the civilian side of the white lines. It is about the players. They are united by this grubbily pure form of football, all of them playing away their strife and worries for a while at least. The final whistle snarls and everyone shakes hands, a mutual respect among the Sunday morning alarm crew. Small wingers climb on buxom centre-halves' shoulders to unhook nets from the crossbar. Boots are heaved off and banged together or clacked against walls, lattices of muck scattering free. Lynx overcomes Ralgex, post-match pubs are chosen. Football at the coalface is a messy community, but a wonderful one.

A green oasis amongst the autumn leaves.

Not everyone watches
as the goals fly in.

Interested human, distracted dog.

Used tape on the crossbar like memories of a summer fiesta.

Balls, water and mud on a cold November Sunday.

The park pavilion, replicated in many parks across the land. This one is the home to Corstorphine Dynamo.

The last ritual as the nets are taken down and stored away.

11

Chapter
12

Tales from the Meadowbank

Charting the loss of Edinburgh's 'other' stadium

"It was one of the worst places that you could play football", says Terry Christie, legendary Meadowbank Thistle manager, when asked about his team's home ground. "That was greatly to our advantage because everybody hated going there. You were distant from the pitch. There was a wind tunnel which came along from Princes Street and down Regent Road and into the stadium, and there was always a gale blowing from west to east that we used to our advantage."

Christie casts these damnations from beneath eyes that beam and twinkle. At this curio of a stadium occurred his greatest footballing days. On that furrowed green noosed by a running track, goals were scored and matches won. Art is possible even on a faulty canvas. His Thistle team, the forgotten younger brother of Auld Reekie football, won promotion and reached a League Cup semi-final with Meadowbank as their home. In 1988, they finished second in Division One but were denied access to the Premier League by a shifting of the deckchairs – aaaaah reconstruction, that old tale with no ending.

Genius of a different type to wily Christie's had previously prettified this turf; in 1971, the Ford Fives European Festival was played here by Matthews and Finney, Puskas and Kubala, and many twinkle-footed more. Inspired, perhaps, Ferranti Thistle moved to the stadium three years later and took Meadowbank as their married name in reverse. This concrete abode was theirs for richer and for poorer. Christie – famed latterly for his duffel coat, as a Beatle was famed for a mop-top or Michael Foot for his donkey jacket – became manager in 1980.

Players rarely loved this place, disliking the music piped into the dressing rooms and their physical separation from supporters by those running lanes. They resented, too, paying 10p to use a communal Edinburgh Council locker for their clothes once they'd changed into their kit. This was a shared space: at 2pm. it belonged to practising long-jumpers; at 3pm to the players of Meadowbank and Stenhousemuir or Dumbarton.

"They putt the shot onto the pitch," remembers Christie, "and things like that, even on a Saturday morning when you're trying to get a smooth pitch. I would go down and take sand out of the sand pit and fill all the holes. You had athletes running on the pitch up to an hour before our games started. One day, it was going on about 45 minutes before kick-off and I went over to them, big guys, and said, "You've got to stop running." I maybe wasn't as diplomatic as I should have been and a guy told me to go to hell. I uttered some oath, at which point this giant of a guy came over and punched me on the chin. Not long until kick-off and I'm lying out on the ground!"

From the deck, Christie would have seen a main stand not unlike those built in the Soviet world. It was a great clump of municipal Brutalism, starkly beautiful – to these eyes anyway – against the repetitive tenements and forever looming and inescapable hills of Edinburgh. Sometimes it is good to not really be sure where you are.

This stadium resembled that of a Warsaw or Leipzig team glimpsed while watching the European Cup Winner's Cup on television. There was the tree-lined exterior that muttered of planned facilities in a Siberian New Town. A colossal scoreboard – shipped here, in fact, from the 1984 Los Angeles Olympics – looked more apt for pronouncements of a Great Leader's triumphs than proclamations of a goal for St Mirren. Bleached orange seats fading like a holiday tan were each stamped with a number in a font that recalled the cumbersome entrance door to a Cold War bunker; in some other version of history, this could well have been home to a military football club bolstered by its doting and controlling state apparatus. And, of course, there was that running track girdling the pitch, a blissfully rare sight in British football, yet one that added to Meadowbank's oddly alluring air of otherness. Here rested a little pocket of Leningrad tucked behind Arthur's Seat.

Now, though, the wrecking ball is poised like a shotputter's arm. Pile drivers wait to pock the surface like fattened javelins. When they wipe this bedraggled oddity from the face of the city, they will erase traces of Christie and Thistle, and of the rising Edinburgh City FC, residents here from 1996 until 2017. The plan is that they will move back some day to another Meadowbank, overshadowed now not by a fascinating outlier of a stadium, but by flats. This is modern Edinburgh, where thin walls reign over interesting ones.

When football stands are bulldozed, they collapse slowly and heavily like afternoon drunks. It is a cruel death. Terraces are difficult to delete. They are stubborn as old dogs and seem to gnarl their teeth at the pneumatic drill. But it will all fall. Even the floodlights will founder. And those of us who know this city will look over one day and feel sad that they are not there. ●

The old north turnstiles which lay unused for decades.

Arthur's Seat looms above the main stand at Meadowbank Stadium.

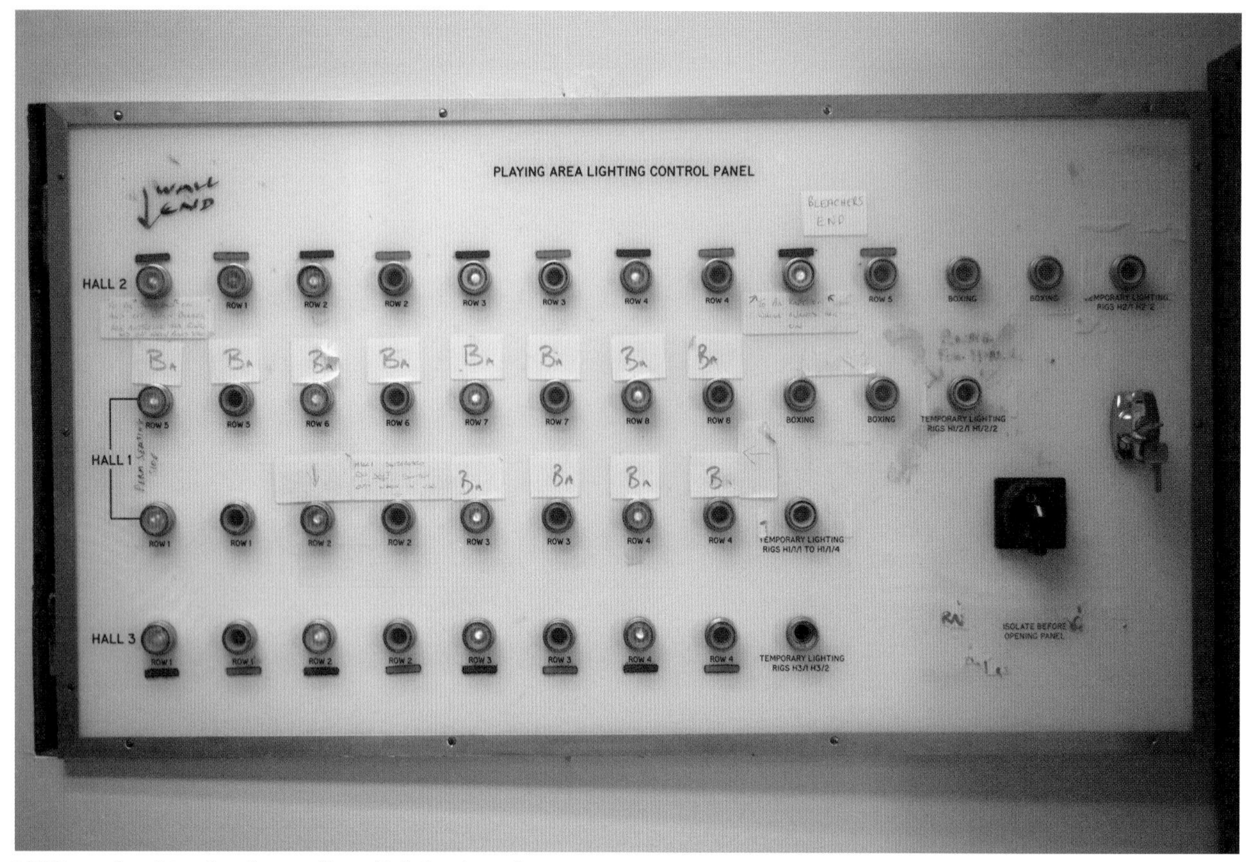

1970s technology for the stadium lighting board.

The stadium flag room.

The main stand which contained shooting galleries beneath the terracing.

The scoreboard was originally used for the 1984 Los Angeles Olympics before being shipped to Meadowbank.

The Brutalist angles of the main stand.

The pylon floodlights.

The geometry of the main stand entrance.

Chapter
13

Darby and Joan football

The Highland League is a glimpse of what this game can be

For a long time I didn't think to ask what it meant. In most of the letters my grandma wrote to me, it was there. "I'm doing my crossword and Grandad's reading the cricket results, right Darby and Joan pair, you know us" and "Well, Grandad's watching his programme and I'm about to put the kettle on, proper Darby and Joan as usual."

One day, years later, suddenly remembering the phrase, I looked it up. "Darby and Joan *n*," said *Chambers Dictionary*, "a devoted elderly married couple". Through further reading and in various conversations over time, I came to understand that Darby and Joan represented quiet contentment and noble serenity. There were no wild highs or catastrophes, few carousals or dramas. A Darby and Joan existence was one out of view, one where sound and fury were absent. Where nothing really happened and yet something universally yearned for was achieved: a happy kind of life. This was exactly how I imagined the Highland League to be. Proper Darby and Joan football.

As we drive north, there is little gentle, content or pleasing about what lurks beside the A9 and then the A95. Here lies roadkill. Every few hundred metres. roadkill in numbers neither of us has ever seen before. Roadkill to make you believe that the apocalypse cometh. It is quite possible to measure speed not in miles covered per hour, but in deceased grouse, rabbits and pheasants spotted per hour. Near Dalnacardoch a perished, colossal badger sprawls across the layby. From a distance, it resembles a football club's furry mascot that has been floored by a stray shot during the warm-up. It reminds us that while spring is about beginnings, it is about endings too. Light kills off dark. Bluebells shoulder-charge snowdrops.

Few lambs make it beyond the slaughterhouse. And the football season ends.

So it is here in Grantown-on-Spey today. The Thistles of Strathspey and Buckie are contesting a final fixture in the Highland League's 34-game season. Outside amiable Seafield Park, home-printed signs in plastic sleeves are tacked to the mesh fence. They proclaim the three items of club merchandise available, pronounce admission prices (£8 and £4, kids go free) and advertise for a new club secretary ("General level of admin/IT skills required" and "Interesting role for a reliable person"). Inside, gents in standard Committee Man regalia loiter and welcome us. They are among the species of great crested suits who keep our game ticking over. Always the club tie, always the shiny lapel pin badge and burnished plain toe shoes.

There is something appealing about huts with hatches in football grounds. Perhaps they awaken a fairground kind of glee. Here, supporters can roll up! roll up! to buy a scarf, pay their way in or enter the half-time 50/50 draw. Each of the booths, we learn, was built by the merry man in charge of admission. His wooden ticket-issuing contraption is a wonder of carpentry. It is to the modern barcode turnstile what a stately grandfather clock is to an Apple Watch. This, of course, is a comforting analogue version of football: no flickering electronic hoardings here, just advertisements for butchers and Cairngorm Concrete – As Hard As The Hills. In such homespun and festive surroundings, perhaps the soundtrack should be chitter-chatter above a tame steam-powered organ. Instead, the air is disturbed and restless. A parcel of oystercatchers pipe their screeched *kleep-kleeps* on continuous loop. The birds have nested on a floodlight and swoop down repeatedly, appearing to dive-bomb Buckie players as they stretch and run between cones.

Perhaps these majestic swoopers have eggs to defend. Perhaps they've seen the roadkill. Tinny Tannoy renditions of football ground staples "I Gotta Feeling" and "Seven Nation Army" croak into life and partially overcome the kleep-kleeps. In the covered seating area, early arrivals Shonagh and Charlie tap their feet and wait for the game. Grantown's Darby and Joan, perhaps. If leaving before the

Improvised seating at Station Park during the Nairn County vs Formartine Utd match.

HOME TEAM
NCFC
1914

The Club '59 supporters of Rothes FC, the best in the Highland League.

end of a game is a sin, then we commit an even greater one – leaving before the game has even started. We have more northern parts to reach.

The A939 to Nairn is another roadkill alley. 'Jesus Saves' reads the graffiti on a boulder up on Dava Moor. Apparently not, suggest the ironed carcasses we witness. At Station Park, the burnt sweetcorn shirts of Nairn County are taking on the barber's pole stripes of Formartine United. We push an ornate old turnstile and enter a cosy ground that feels like a society all of its own. There is a hatch selling products from the local bakery and various outbuildings, one of which appears to be a crèche. A brand new toilet block is testament to what another Committee Man in standard livery tells us: "We prefer to spend money on our supporters." He has worked that turnstile for half a century. I recall that Nairn County once joined with the local Citizens Advice Bureau to attack payday loan companies and offer debtors help. Football as a force for good – I like the sound of that.

On the grassy knoll behind a goal and in the two sideline stands, the atmosphere of community continues. Kids run about, play football themselves and jeer misguided Formartine shots. Adults stand and gesticulate about the game or sit on benches and talk about football, life, whatever.

I watch a father remark upon the game to his son, but not in the occasional, catchphrase manner of the standard issue Scottish football dad with his bile yer heid referees and och wheesht opponents. His conversation is constant, descriptive, unyielding; steady verses for build-up play rising to bold choruses for shots on goal. Moving nearer, I see that the two are standing close together, tight as matchsticks in a box. Dad is white-haired, son in early middle age. Though blind, through his father's words he never misses a kick, hack or tantrum. Here is unbound affection – for football, yes, but most of all between a papa and his boy. Halos fuzz

Over the wall. Nairn County supporters at Station Park, Nairn.

abovc humanity in thc most unlikcly of places. Even football grounds.

This place is everything our game can be. Here, it is seagulls that bother ears, but they are overcome by raucous home supporters. The football is frenetic and yet laboured. When United, 30-odd points above County, miss a penalty, there is pantomime elation. It sounds defiant, us-against-the-world, the bond of the put-upon underdog. "You're useless, referee," cries one main stand voice, "and you're bald."

Onwards we must roll in search of the last few minutes of the last day of the season. We stop at well-kempt Mosset Park to pay homage to Forres Mechanics. The Can-Cans are away scoring a halfdozen in Fort William. Walking around an empty football ground is a confidential kind of delight, like a shower late at night. Scents dropping in from the Benromach Distillery over the road make for a quietly intoxicating few minutes. The A941 proffers yet more still game and delivers us in Rothes. Beyond cask warehouses and yards filled with copper pot stills we find Mackessack Park, home to Rothes FC. These tangerines bought floodlights from Tannadice and adopted Dundee United colours too.

In all of our Highland League grounds, it has been difficult to focus on the turf and not the world beyond – at Seafield Park the Hills of Cromdale, at Nairn County the handsome Victorian railway station and here the rich and rolling countryside. "There are worse places to watch football, Murdo," says a man leaning against the Perspex dugout. The final whistle shrills, hands clap and studs clack on cement floors. Supporters amble and meander away in a rather directionless manner, as if their purpose has suddenly been lost or their batteries removed. At the catering hatch, a woman wipes the surface clean and pulls down a shutter. Another Committee Man bolts closed the club shop shed. Football will sleep now until August. "Well, that's the season done, can you believe it?" asks a man in the land of Darby and Joan football.

Shonagh and Charlie Thomson, early arrivals for the Strathspey Thistle v Buckie Thistle match.

The final whistle has blown on the last game of the season at Rothes FC's Mackessack Park, and all that remains is to check the other scores.

The ticket booth at Seafield Park, Grantown-on-Spey, home of Strathspey Thistle.

The Rothes FC club shop is locked for the final time as another Highland League campaign comes to an end.

JGW
SINCLAIR TAYLOR
SPOT ON CABS
moorings mediquip group
WHEELCHAIR CARE
mobility & independent living centre
01309 676677
www.wheelchaircare.co.uk
Xeretec
www.xeretec.co.uk
01463 725 999
REFRESHMENTS
ALWAYS BAKED FROM SCRATCH
SKIP HIRE

No match today. An away fixture for Forres Mechanics sees their home ground of Mosset Park quiet at 3pm on a Saturday afternoon.

In conversation after Rothes FC's final match of the season.

Deep in whisky country, the copper stills overlook Mackessack Park in Rothes, by the banks of the Spey.

The main stand at Seafield Park, Grantown-on-Spey, home of Strathspey Thistle.

The turnstiles at Mosset Park, home of Forres Mechanics FC.

Chapter
14

Silent Saturday

Football's sudden halt when Covid-19 struck

It was everywhere and then it was nowhere. On Thursday we talked of play-offs and calf strains. By Friday football had been shushed. Via a few necessarily cold press releases, Saturday plans were cancelled and the right to cheer or barrack revoked. Here was an act of larceny that we absorbed and agreed with, as if a benevolent burglar were taking away a prized possession for our own good. All we could do was sigh, look to the floor and mutter "I understand, I understand" over and over like a schoolchild being scolded.

Come Saturday, we pondered the empty stadiums with their quarantined goalmouths. We thought of majestic old Cappielow, wind roaming unchallenged along its terraces. We thought of lofty St James' Park, a Goliath with nothing to look down upon. We thought of homely Fratton Park, a screaming banshee of a ground now quieter than Christmas Day on the moon. Of course, these places are empty and silent most of the time, yet this was a starving kind of gap and a denser, more potent quiet. It was different. Games were supposed to be happening right there, right then. Now, we did not know when they would take place, if at all.

We thought too, of those grounds' surroundings: the pubs that half-rely on fortnightly splurges of lager and crisps, the social clubs with their untouched buffets under cling film. Then there were the programmes, bundled, tied and going nowhere. Collectors' items, perchance? Floodlights rested their eyes and padlocks handcuffed catering hatches. On this late winter's Saturday, nothing glowed except the odd good deed in a weary world; some clubs gave matchday food to the local needy, a feast sent from No Man's Land.

It was easy to spot people who were supposed to be at a game. They walked eerie streets and sat in tetchy pubs, heads down and thoughts vacant. Every now and then, they would forget themselves and habits would spur an outbreak of automatic behaviour: fingers sliding to latest-score apps; minds wondering how Ipswich Town were getting on; a quick check in the paper to see what the Sunday 4pm fixture was. Some switched to Sky Sports News in the hope of finding Jeff Stelling

Everything is silent at Cappielow Park, home of Greenock Morton.

announcing that Falkirk had taken the lead at Dumbarton.

On Sunday, it seemed to sink in. Numb acceptance spread. There were no scores pages to devour, no defeats to wallow in. In the evening, there was no *Match of the Day 2* or *Sportscene* closing theme tune to lull us off to bed. Our scarves, we realised, were sentenced to an unhealthy term on the peg. Hymns would go unsung. And how we would miss that very act of communal singing, something we simply do not do elsewhere. Our therapy sessions had expired.

It was not like pre-season, with its steady course to August through transfer speculation, friendly matches and new kits. Fixtures faded from the canvas rather than appearing in fresh paint. Football had no cheery shop-window note declaring "Back in 5 minutes". All we knew was that it would return. And when it did, hell, that first goal would feel better than it had for years.

Some weeks later, it was as if the sky knew that football had ceased. Gone for days on end were the clouds. The sun hung over us unremitting, loyal and somehow sinister. Rain was something from *before all this*, like pubs and handshakes. Football weather, with its damp Aprils and viciously cold May Saturdays, had departed on the coattails of the sport itself.

Once it vanished, neighbours, acquaintances or in-laws could no longer ask how our teams were faring. Footballing small talk came now through a question asked of our partners over telephones and online portals: "How is he coping without the football?" From some this was heartfelt, expressed in the same concerned tone with which one might enquire about the health of a poorly pet cat. From others, scorn or a roll of the eyes could be detected, as if going without football were as inconsequential as going without eggs or compost.

How we felt did matter, though. Missing football is an important, valid emotion. It did not mean that we lacked perspective or that we did not cry the same distressed tears as others during news bulletins. We supporters know how far down the list of importance football is, and very few fans wished for matches to happen again until they could be played safely, and with us there. But we should never have felt the need to apologise for the brittle moments when a piece of music or the smell of grass reminded us of matchday and what had evaporated.

The very act of going to a game matters tremendously. It matters to your routine, identity and equilibrium, and it matters to the routine, identity and equilibrium of so many thousands of others. It is making the same journey, meeting the same Saturday friends, filing along the same row past the same grumbling owners of immovable knees to take your seat, or landing in the same spot on the sainted terrace. Then, it is seeing those colours you love and letting those who wear them infuriate, exult and disappoint you all over again. Our grounds mattered in all of this too – suddenly, we were exiled from our second homes.

Through most of April's perturbingly clement afternoons, my daughter and I opened our house's upstairs windows and sat looking at the gardens beneath us. Most days, outside a house four or five along, a teenage boy played football with his mum. Their laughter and the heavenly sound of a football bouncing washed pleasantly upwards. Beyond the rooftops, we looked to the pleasant green arms and prongs of Easter Road Stadium, half-checking it still existed.

One day in May, a funeral cortege crawled by that stadium. The family of the deceased – Gordon "Gogsy" Reid, taken by Covid-19 aged 68 – had asked that his hearse pass by the places he loved most in life. A hundred or so people stood outside the Famous Five Stand, applauding this dearly loved man at two-metre intervals. "Farewell for now, Gogs," said his brother-in-law during a eulogy at Mortonhall Crematorium, "See you behind the goals. You get the pies, I'll get the Bovril." ●

Hibernian's Easter Road Stadium soars above the tenements in the Leith sunshine.

Daniel Gray is a writer and broadcaster based in Leith. Born in the north-east of England, he grew up in York and moved to Scotland in 2004. He is the author of nine other books, and Editor of Nutmeg magazine, for whom he is also podcast producer/presenter. He is producer/ presenter of the When Saturday Comes magazine podcast, and writes across a number of newspapers and other media. Daniel has been appearing on radio and television for over a decade, and has also been writer/researcher on a number of BBC and STV documentary series. He is happiest looking out of a train window on his way to an obscure football match, or watching Middlesbrough FC with his daughter.

Alan McCredie is a photographer, lecturer and film maker. A Perthshire lad lost to Edinburgh, he supports St Johnstone FC. He is the photographer/ author of six previous books, including the Saltire-nominated This is Scotland with Daniel Gray, My Scotland with Val McDermid and Scotland the Dreich. His portrait and documentary work has appeared in a number of exhibitions over the years, and his epic 100 Weeks of Scotland project saw him take different images of this country in the two years leading up to the 2014 independence referendum. Alan lectures at Edinburgh College of Art and lives in Leith. In their photo essays, he and Daniel are driven by a passion to find the perfect chip butty.

What is Nutmeg?
Nutmeg is our game, in print.
Published every three months,
it is a high-class home for quality
articles about Scottish football's
past, present and future.
It offers opinion, reflection,
interviews, insight, illustration,
photography and poetry.
It is a unique blend between
196 uniquely elegant pages.

Subscribe:
www.nutmegmagazine.co.uk
It's our game.
In print.
On podcasts.
At events.

Typography
Logotype: Breve Display Regular.
Body text: Acta Roman.
Headlines: Acta Display Black.
All by Dino Dos Santos
DSType Foundry. www.dstype.com